How to

OWN YOUR HOME

Years Sooner &

Retire Debt FREE

By Harj Gill (M.Ed)

www.SpeedEquity.com

How To Own Your Home Years Sooner & Retire Debt FREE

ISBN   978-0-9850603-1-2

First Published in Australia January 1997
Revised Australian Edition June 1997
Revised Australian Edition May 1998
Revised Australian Edition November 1999
Revised Australian Edition May 2000
Revised Australian Edition September 2000
Revised Australian Edition November 2000
Revised Australian Edition September 2001
Revised Australian Edition September 2002
Revised Australian Edition May 2014
Revised Australian Edition January 2016

First North American Edition November 2003
Revised North American Edition April 2004
Revised North American Edition May 2014
Revised North American Edition August 2018
Revised North American Edition August 2019

What the experts have said ...

"... it's a BRILLIANT system."

• NBC's "Saving You Money"

"... shows how you can cut the term of your home loan significantly."

• Personal Investment Magazine

"Save a bundle on your home loan."

• The Sunday Times

"... this book is an excellent summary and detailed analysis of methods by which mortgages can be effectively eliminated."

• WA Business News

"... gives us hope that we can achieve freedom from our mortgage before a ripe old age."

• Your Mortgage Magazine

"It's like having your money do aerobics."

• Mortgage Know How Magazine

"Strategies for saving a bundle on home loans."

• The Melbourne Age

"This book shows you step-by-step how you can own your home years sooner."

• Perth Woman Magazine

"Save thousands on your home loan."

• The Australian Women's Weekly

What readers are saying ...

Contents

Acknowledgments

For my wife and daughter … my Sun and my Moon.

Read Me First

Hello, my name is Harj Gill and I am the creator of the Speed Equity® Mortgage Acceleration System.

Before I delve into the subject matter at hand, please allow me to share with you a little background about myself, and the turbulent beginnings of this revolutionary System. It's especially important for you to know that bankers and lenders don't like me. They don't like me because I teach ordinary people, families just like yours, how to take full mathematical advantage of a little known Key Banking Principle that lenders DON'T want you to know about. A SECRET so powerful that it can help you slash years off your home loan and save you tens to hundreds of thousands of dollars in interest.

Next, I am an teacher and … what I have done since I created this System, way back in 1996, is to educate and empower over half a million homeowners, in eight different countries to be able to Own Their Homes Years Sooner & Retire Debt Free.

How it all started

I have always had a curious nature and a strong desire to understand the world around me from a clinical, logical, and practical perspective. Therefore, it was only natural that I gravitated to the hard sciences whereby I attended the University of Western Australia and graduated with a Bachelor of Science Degree and a Postgraduate Diploma in Science.

I then went on to get a Masters Degree specializing in an area called "Organizational Planning and Change". The latter qualification gave me the perfect foundation to put my curiosity and analytical mind to full use.

In essence, I am academically trained as a research analyst. My specialty is to collect and evaluate seemingly unrelated data from the broader environment and present my findings to corporate executives.

My real talent lies in packaging that information in the form of emerging trends along with recommendations and strategies to help make a company more profitable. In other words, I'm a numbers nerd. In fact, I love numbers so much that I was at the top of my statistics class at university.

In 1995, while working as an organizational consultant, I came across a little known Key Banking Principle that governs how interest on a mortgage is calculated and charged. When I applied my academic research skills to this subject, I grasped that if I could teach ordinary home loan borrowers how to take full mathematical advantage of this Key Banking Principle, they could literally slash years off their home loans and save tens to hundreds of $1,000's in interest.

To cut a long story short, this discovery forced me to make a conscious decision to leave the world of organizational consulting. I realized that instead of helping faceless corporations make more profits, I could use this newfound knowledge to make a huge difference in the lives of real people. So, I decided to develop the Speed Equity® Mortgage Acceleration System. This System was, and still is, considered revolutionary because it shows borrowers how to significantly reduce the interest cost on their mortgage simply by using their existing financial resources. That's right! It's not about working harder, but working SMARTER with the money you already have right now.

As I started teaching people how to use this System, I soon found that it was completely transforming their lives. I witnessed first hand, as people felt the burden of a 30-year mortgage being lifted, that their thinking began to change also. I saw them get giddily excited about the very tangible prospect of Owning Their Homes Years Sooner & Retiring Debt Free.

For many, it was the first time they had ever taken complete control of their financial future. And for the first time, they knew exactly WHAT they needed to do, HOW they were going to do it, and EXACTLY where they should be each step of the way. As a result, they started to dream about making new plans for their future. They began to live the life they *WANTED to live* rather than living the life they thought they *HAD to live*. In this book I am going to introduce you to some of these people that all started where you are today. None of them are famous or overly wealthy. In fact, they are just ordinary people who no longer wanted to be enslaved by a 30-year mortgage and made the simple decision to break free from it. For example:

- Bill and Greta who had a 25-year mortgage and reduced it to 12-years 7-months AND saved $93,773 in interest.

- David & Sheryl, a single income couple that reduced their 20-year 4-month mortgage to 9-years 11-months AND saved $83,216 in interest.

- Simon & Fiona, a young working couple who paid off their 13-year 2 month mortgage in 5-years and 11-months AND saved $84,847 in interest.

As I have come to expect, the initial reaction of every one of these people when they found out just how quickly they could pay off their home loans was, *"I don't believe it!"* However, after only the first month of following their personalized Speed Equity® Plans, they were achieving their forecasted results and well on their way to Owning Their Homes Years Sooner & Retiring Debt Free. While reading this book, you too will learn the simple step-by-step process of what these people did to dramatically reduce the term of their home loans so you too can do the same.

No one wants to read about a "math-problem"

When I saw the extraordinary results my 1-on-1 coaching clients were achieving, I wanted to share my knowledge and case studies with as many people as possible. In order to do that, I knew I had to put everything I discovered and learned into a medium that was readily accessible AND affordable by everyone. The logical step was to write a book. Consequently, the first edition of this book was self-published in Australia, in January 1997.

Why was it self-published?

Because when I submitted my original manuscript to the major publishing houses in Australia at the time, they told me in no uncertain terms that; *"No one wants to read about a math problem!"*

Fortunately for me, I found that a lot of people ARE INTERESTED in reading about a "math problem" - especially if it can save them tens to hundreds of $1,000's in interest and slash years off their mortgage. The testament to that came in February 1997, a month after my first print edition. That's when the producers of a National Investigative Current Affairs TV Program called "Today Tonight", much like "20/20" and "Dateline NBC", contacted me. They asked to interview me about my book and System along with people using it. This System was so controversial and revolutionary that they aired the story on prime time National TV straight after the six o'clock news.

Much to their delight, it generated the highest ratings in the history of that program. From that point forward, I went on to receive extensive media coverage throughout Australia. Incidentally, you can watch these TV interviews along with the ones from the U.S. (when I was featured on NBC's "Saving You Money") on my website ... **www.SpeedEquity.com**

Why lenders DON'T want you to know about this System

A lot of trusting souls still insist on saying to me, *"If your System is so good, then why hasn't my bank told me about it?"*

The short and simple answer to that question is because they stand to lose billions of dollars in interest if they were to do so. In fact, this is such a threatening concept to their bottom line that staff at some of the biggest banks in Australia actively tried to discredit me and my System when my original book was launched there in 1997 ... more about that in a moment.

You see, the job of every good banker is to maximize profits for their shareholders. And the way they do that is to sell you a 30-year mortgage so they can keep charging you interest for all those years. If all of a sudden they start teaching you how to pay off your 30-year mortgage in a third or even half the time, just imagine what it would do to their bottom line. For example, based on the latest data I gathered from home loan borrowers that are using this System, the average amount of time and interest they are saving on a 30-year mortgage is as follows ...

Average Interest Saving:	= $109,293
Average Time Saving:	= 16 years

Now you do the math

Multiply these savings by 100,000 homeowners and you have nearly $11 BILLION in saved/lost interest depending on whether you are a borrower or a lender. Even if the average interest savings were only $10,000 per homeowner, that still equates to over $1 billion in lost interest ... not exactly the results a bank executive wants to take back and present to his/her stockholders. Let me share with you a personal anecdote about this ...

Back in the summer of 2004, I was invited to present this System to the entire management team of a bank who were gathered at the Annual Mortgage Bankers' Association Convention in San Diego, CA. The invite was at the behest of the head of marketing for this particular bank - who thought this System would really give his bank an edge in the consumer lending market. So, he asked me to fly down from Seattle, WA (where I am based), to meet the CEO and his team.

On the day of the presentation, I was picked up in a flashy town car from my hotel and chauffeur driven to the venue. So there I am, in one of the best boardrooms at the conference venue, dressed in my best suit and tie. I was ready to dazzle them with how this System would help their bank make record profits by creating a unique value proposition that says; "At XYZ bank, we'll not only help you find the best home loan ... we'll show you how to pay it off years sooner as well."

I began my presentation with the customary background and history and I'm no more than seven minutes into explaining this concept when the CEO, who shall remain nameless to protect the guilty, stops me dead in my tracks. Here's how the conversation unfolded from there ...

Bank CEO: *"Mr. Gill I get it!"* (I guess that's why he was the CEO).

"This is a BRILLIANT concept. But how do you expect me to explain to my stockholders that they're going to lose tens of millions, if not hundreds of millions, in profits in the next quarter if we start telling all our customers about it?"

Me: *"Mr. XXX, I completely understand your concerns and it's not the first time I've been met with that objection from someone in your position. You see, what I'm advocating here is a long-term strategy that will not only increase your profits, but will set you apart from every other mortgage lender in the country."*

"By showing your clients How to Own Their Homes Years Sooner with this System, you will not only have them paying back their mortgages in record time, which means lower default rates, but they will most likely "move up" into a bigger home or be in a position to purchase a second home much sooner than they had anticipated." Before he had a chance to interrupt, I continued ...

"Furthermore, If you do the right thing by your customers by giving them the right loan products to implement this System, you will not only have a client for an entire lifetime, but they will most likely recommend you to everyone they know because of what you did for them."

"Yes, there is potential for reduction in short term profits. However, you will more than make up for it by capturing a large market share, reduced delinquencies, lower acquisition costs due to repeat and referral business as well as generating immeasurable goodwill by sending a message to every homeowner in this country that you are on their side."

Bank CEO: *"I see your point Mr. Gill. But it still comes down to my bank's profit margins and I'm not willing to take that risk."*

"Thank you for your time and I wish you the best of luck."

Well, I wasn't surprised at his response because as I said, it was not the first time I had heard such an objection. But, it did give me a chance to visit the lovely city of San Diego, CA.

Incidentally, according to the U.S. Census Bureau, there were an estimated 49.325 million housing units with a mortgage in 2011. If only 1% of these homeowners decided to implement this System, that would equate to over $49 BILLION in lost interest. Now do you see why your lender has absolutely no vested interest in telling you about it?

I'd like to finish this section with one more anecdote from my Australian experience that will bring home to you what an uphill battle it has been trying to work with lenders and ... some of the obstacles you too may experience when dealing with them in trying to implement this System.

"We shall NOT be a part of any such scheme!"

As I mentioned, this book and System made their debut on a national current affairs TV program in Australia ... February 10th, 1997 to be exact. When that happened, the book immediately became a bestseller with thousands of copies being sold in the first week and people rushing to their banks in droves demanding the types of mortgages in accordance with the characteristics I recommended in it.

Sadly, most were met with staunch skepticism and disbelief from the lending staff themselves. They were told that such a system could not possibly work and that it was a scam. Furthermore, in all of that time, I only had one customer ever ask for their money back, and that was way back in 1997. I was so taken aback that I kept the handwritten letter for all of these years. Here is a scan of the letter explaining why this customer, a Mrs. C.E. Tranent, wanted a refund ... and because it may be difficult to read, I have transcribed the entire text on the next page.

Australian Mortgage
Reduction Specialists.
P.O. Box 72
West Perth.
W.A. 6872.

Dear Sir

I first viewed your segment on "The Kerri-Anne Kennely Show" and was excited by the chance to own my home years sooner through your promoted scheme

I phoned the number stated on the show and was assured that our bank "Commonwealth" was and would be prepared to negotiate a similar scheme of repayments for me.

Since recieving your booklet and other information leaflets. I phoned "The Commonwealth" and was informed that they would not be part of any such scheme

Today 2-6-97. I phoned your freecall helpline 1800 628 729. Explained my dilema to your consultant and was adviced to return the pack to recieve a full refund. This I have done.

Would you please credit my ——————————— with $39.95 as promised.

Yours faithfully

C. d. Tranent

Mrs. C.E. Tranent.

Dear Sir,

I first viewed your segment on "The Kerry-Anne Kennely Show" (**national TV talk show in Australia**) and was excited by the chance to own my home years sooner through your promoted scheme.

I phoned the number on the show and was assured that our bank 'Commonwealth' (**second largest bank in Australia**) was and would be prepared to negotiate a similar scheme of repayments for me.

Since receiving your booklet and other information leaflets, I phoned 'The Commonwealth' and was informed that **they would not be part of any such scheme.**

Today 2-6-97 (2nd June, 1997) I phoned your freecall helpline xxxx xxx xxx (Australia only) explained my dilemma to your consultant and was advised to return the book to receive a full refund. This I have done.

Would you please credit my Master Card No xxxx xxxx xxxx with $39.95 as promised

Yours faithfully,

Mrs. C.E. Tranent

The irony of it all is that five years later (2002), the bank in question developed a home loan product directly in accordance with my criteria for the types of mortgages to use with the Speed Equity® Mortgage Acceleration System, and then heavily promoted it using the language from my book.

Take a look at the copy of the bank's ad on the next page and read the wording. Notice any similarities with their ad and what you've been reading in this book so far?

Poor old Mrs. Tranent.

I sometimes wonder how she's doing. She could have been 5-years closer to owning her home had her bank allowed her to "Make it happen" as they later claimed in their national advertising campaign for their "new" loan product.

The Commonwealth Bank advertisement in the
Sunday Times on July 14, 2002

1. Compared to a standard home loan a Viridian Line of Credit Home Loan is a flexible, all-in-one account that builds equity faster by reducing your loan balance, twenty-four hours a day, seven days a week.

2. By depositing your salary and savings into Viridian you automatically reduce your loan balance and the amount of daily interest owing.

3. Having your Commonwealth Bank Credit Card linked to Viridian means you can use your credit card to make your day-to-day purchases. Each month your entire credit card balance can be swept to your Viridian account. This lets you take advantage of the 'up to 55 days interest-free period' on your credit card, saving you even more in interest costs.

4. Viridian also lets you use the equity built up in your home to fund other investments (like property, shares or managed funds) at home loan rates.

5. Plus, you have the choice of competitive interest rate options.

Make it happen.

What does all this historical background have to do with you?

The point I want to make here is that if you want to Own Your Home Years Sooner & Retire Debt Free, then one of the first things you have to do is get away from the notion that your lender has your best interest at heart. Furthermore, you have to acknowledge these cold, hard facts:

FACT #1: Your lender is an impersonal, for-profit institution. And like any faceless corporation, their sole objective, and right, is to make a profit.

FACT #2: Your lender is NOT a charity organization and is NOT obliged to tell or teach you how to become mortgage free.

Therefore, if I am going to be remotely successful in helping you Own Your Home Years Sooner & Retire Debt Free, then the first thing you MUST realize - AND - accept are the cold, hard facts above.

I can also tell you with 100% certainty that after you finish reading this book you will know more about how to use the banking system to save tens to hundreds of $1,000's in interest on your mortgage than 99.999% of bankers, loan officers, and mortgage brokers out there.

Why? Because they have never been educated like you are about to be. These people are kept in the dark and told to tow the corporate line, which is to sell you a 30-year mortgage ... NOT to help you pay it off years sooner! On that note, I have had veteran bankers and loan officers with twenty plus years experience attend my seminars and say; "WOW! I never knew this."

Having said all that, you will be happy to know that as someone else once said (apparently Abraham Lincoln said it, but it can't be confirmed) ...

"You can fool some of the people some of the time, but you can't fool all of the people all of the time."

Thanks to all the publicity I received in Australia, it allowed me to reach out to and empower over half a million homeowners in that country ... a 25% market penetration into mortgaged households no less. All that people power caused nothing short of a banking revolution over there.

Inadvertently, my readers and I started a grassroots consumer movement that put tremendous pressure on lenders and forced them to develop specialized mortgage products that allowed borrowers to apply the principles of the Speed Equity® Mortgage Acceleration System. The outcome was that in order to retain their existing customers and to stay competitive, almost every lender in that country had to comply with this demand. It wasn't because they wanted to do it. It's just that they were forced to do it through sheer consumer pressure.

Case in point: in 2003 I was approached by the Australian subsidiary of HSBC, a multinational banking consortium headquartered in the UK. At the time it was also the third largest bank in the world with assets of over $1 Trillion. HSBC had developed a new home loan called "Home Smart" and wanted to do a nationwide launch of this product. Their advertising agency at the time contacted my office and asked if they could use my book to promote it. The reason they gave was that it was in complete alignment with the accelerated mortgage reduction principles of my System. I told them I would only say "yes" if their loan product met my criteria and was truly beneficial to consumers.

After carrying out my own due diligence I discovered that it was indeed a great loan product and would help borrowers easily implement this System. As a result, I was happy to give HSBC Australia permission to use my book to promote their "Home Smart" home loan.

In the years that have since passed, my book and Speed Equity® Software Program have received rave reviews from every financial publication and expert that reviewed them. Today, borrowers as far as Malaysia, Singapore, South Africa, Canada, New Zealand, the UK and the United States are using the Speed Equity® Mortgage Acceleration System. I just wanted to share this information with you so you have some general background about me, my journey to get this System into the hands of homeowners, and how long it has been around.

Now, you are about to learn the huge impact it has had on the lives of hundreds of thousands of people using it. As a result, today, you are holding the 4th revised U.S. edition in your hot little hands and the 10th Australian edition has just gone to print.

So much for people not being interested in a math problem!

I want to finish this chapter by saying that I feel extremely fortunate to do something I love dearly and ... to have had the privilege of reaching out to and making a positive difference in the lives of so many people. To that end, I am deeply honored that you are taking the time to read this book and my desire is to make a huge difference in your life as well.

A word to the wise

Before you go on, it is important for you to immediately realize what my System and book are *not*.

First, my System is not a 'get-rich-quick' scheme. There are a host of hucksters out there that have jumped on my bandwagon claiming to have "created" mortgage acceleration programs and software. Almost all of them are in it to make a quick buck by robbing you of thousands of dollars because they know how to take advantage of peoples' ignorance about mortgages. There's one particular company that wants you to completely Replace Your Mortgage with a first lien HELOC and expose your entire home loan to the variable interest rate. For that privilege, you can expect to pay up to $4,000 and put your entire financial future in jeopardy. I'll elaborate on this insane strategy later in this book. However that's not the kind of B.S. (Blue Sky) you will find in this book.

What you will find however, are fundamental Mathematical and Banking Principles that only the wealthy and very top bankers know about and have been keeping to themselves ever since the advent of credit.

Second, this is not another dry, stuffy textbook about personal finance (as you are discovering). I want you to know that there is a real person who put this whole System together, and that's me. I deal with *real* people, in the *real* world, and I want to communicate my ideas to you in a fun and relaxed way as if you were sitting right across the table from me.

I also want to mention that *all* of the information in this book has grown out of my own personal experience and my consulting activities. Nearly all of the people I will refer to in this book have saved at least $50,000 in interest on their home loans - some over half a million dollars in interest. You will also note that this edition is infused with a little international flavor in terms of the anecdotes and some of the language I use due to the broad range of homeowners from all the different countries that I have had the privilege of working with.

Last, I call this edition my *POLITICALLY INCORRECT, NO HOLDS BARRED, TELL IT LIKE IT IS EDITION*. My first and foremost objective is to educate and empower you. I want for you to make informed decisions and I'm not going to sugarcoat anything. I just wanted to put that on the table so you understand and appreciate the value of what you are holding in your hands. It's equivalent to a personal consultation of at least $5,000 with me and collectively represents billions of dollars in interest savings by hundreds of thousands of people just like you. And all these people did was to make the decision to apply in their lives the knowledge and tools I will share with you.

If you diligently put into practice the information in this book and on my website, you too will be well on your way to slashing years off your home loan and saving tens to hundreds of $1,000's in interest. So sit back and enjoy learning how to make your money work harder for you because that is definitely something your banker will not be running out the door to help you do. Now let's begin the journey of helping you Own Your Home Years Sooner & Retiring Debt Free shall we?

> *"Make it a must that whenever you hear about something,*
> *read, or research something you think has value for your Life,*
> *DON'T let it become just knowledge.*
> **Convert it into action.**
> *For it is through our actions that our destiny is shaped."*
> - Anthony Robbins -

Chapter 1
Why You Should Own Your Home Years Sooner As An American

*"One of the true tests of Leadership is the ability,
to recognize a problem before it becomes an emergency."*

- Arnold H. Glasow -

Our inevitable future

Although my obvious goal is to help you Own Your Home Years Sooner & Retire Debt Free, my underlying motivation in developing the Speed Equity® Mortgage Acceleration System has always been much more profound and subtle. You see, I want you to go way beyond owning your home to developing a "wealthy mindset" and become financially free as well.

Now why do I want you to do that? Why do I want you to retire financially independent rather than simply stopping at paying off your mortgage and your debts? The answers to this question should set off huge alarm bells for you because here is ...

The state of our nation in terms of retirement planning

- Only about half of American workers have a retirement plan. Of those with a 401(k), many don't participate (Money, March 2009).

- 82% of employers who sponsor 401(k) plans say most of their employees will not be adequately prepared for retirement (USA Today, Oct. 2008).

- 4-in-10 working Americans say they will never be able to afford to retire (Harris Interactive Survey, April 2011).

- 72% do not think it is possible for a middle-income family to save for a secure retirement, up from 70% who thought this in 2010 and 63% in 2007 (Country Financial Survey, April 2011).

- An analysis of 10,000 accounts revealed that the average 401(k) participant needs to work until 73 to afford retirement (NyHart: Employee Benefits Consulting Firm, December 2010).

- After 20-years of "Fun & Easy" retirement education workshops and seminars, studies show that the great majority of employees now in their 60's have less than $100,000 in their 401(k)s. That amounts to $333/month at a 4% annual withdrawal (Defined Contribution Insights, May/June 2009). Consequently ...

- Nearly two-thirds of baby boomers surveyed said Social Security will either be an "extremely" or "very" important source of income when they retire (Poll conducted by the Associated Press and the LifeGoesStrong.com lifestyle website in April 2011). This last statistic is extremely alarming because ...

Social Security? Medicare? ... What's that?

Pretty soon we will all be asking that very same question.

In the very first American edition of this book (Nov. 2003), I warned readers about what was fast approaching down the pike for this great country of ours in terms of its financial future. Back then I quoted from a press release issued by the Board of Trustees for the US Social Security System on March 17, 2003. The headline read, *"Social Security is NOT Sustainable for the Long Term."* In their annual report tabled at Congress, the trustees announced that there were only enough funds to sustain Social Security payments for another 39-years, and that Medicare would be completely bankrupt within the next 23-years. The 2012 Trustees Report delivered even worse news. It is now projected that:

- The Medicare trust fund will run out of money in 2024 under current projections - two years earlier than expected in 2003.

- The news for Social Security is even direr. The combined trust fund that holds funding reserves for the overall Social Security program is now expected to run out of money in 2033 - a full nine years earlier than projected in 2003.

Another way to look at this is if you were 40-years old in 2012, then Medicare will be bankrupt by the time you reach age 52, and you can no longer rely on Social Security after the age of 61. And yet, we (and soon our children) are all required to contribute to it with no hope of gaining any benefit. Didn't they put a guy called Bernie Madoff in prison for running something called a "Ponzi Scheme"?

Personally, I estimate these cataclysmic financial events will occur sooner than predicted thanks to almost a trillion dollars of tax payer money the government handed out to bailout Wall Street and the financial system that got us into a bigger mess. Not to mention the government's debt in December 2012 of nearly $16.4 Trillion ... the largest of any nation in history and with no signs of slowing. Furthermore, I have a sneaky suspicion that we are not being told the true state of economic affairs because everyone wants to carry on as if it's business as usual to avoid mass panic.

Now, given the last set of data I shared with you regarding the state of retirement planning for this country, the number of boomers that are going to rely on social security as an important part of their income, the abysmal state of Social Security and Medicare, ask yourself; *"What future do I foresee for this country and what measures would our government have to set in motion to accommodate this impending future that is now upon us?"*

You see, once you collect all the data and connect the dots, the seemingly unrelated data points start to make sense and you begin to arrive at some very obvious and disturbing conclusions. Welcome to my world of being a "numbers nerd". In case you're not convinced to take action just yet, here's something really scary ...

Court sets precedence: approves termination of pension fund

You may not be aware but there was a frightening precedence set on May 11, 2005, by Federal Bankruptcy Judge Eugene Wedoff, when he ruled that United Airlines could default on its pension obligations. At the time, United Airlines' $9.8 billion pension plan default was the largest in U.S. history. Affecting more than 120,000 employees, it resulted in many workers losing as much as half of their allotted pension. That single action left the gates wide open for any corporation to walk away from their retirement benefits obligations like pension and health care plans.

For those of you thinking the Pension Benefit Guaranty Corporation (PBGC) will come to our rescue, think again. FYI: the PBGC is an independent agency of the U.S. government. It was created by the Employee Retirement Income Security Act of 1974 (ERISA) to encourage the continuation and maintenance of voluntary private defined benefit pension plans. In 2010 the agency said its total obligations were $102.5 billion and only $79.5 billion in assets to pay for those obligations. In other words, the PBGC is already broke.

Meanwhile public sector employees are not faring any better either. A lot of them make the mistake of thinking that just because they work for "the government", that somehow their financial future will be more secure - not so. State and local pension funds comprise a patchwork of 2,700 funds that manage $1.4 Trillion on behalf of 21-million public employees, including teachers, firefighters, policemen and other municipal workers. A sampling of these funds revealed that statistically, a lot of them are under-funded, meaning that they would not be able to pay the future benefits promised.

On March 04, 2013, Reuters released an article titled, **"U.S. state pension funding gap up 20 percent in 2012."** These are direct quotes from that article:

> *"The shortfall in 109 of the nation's state pension plans rose to $834.2 billion in 2012, up from $690.3 billion the previous year, according to a new report by Wilshire Consulting, a unit of independent investment management firm Wilshire Associates.*

> *"Of 109 state plans, 95 percent are underfunded, with asset values less than their liabilities. The average underfunded plan has a ratio of assets to liabilities of just 68 percent.*

> *"The problem varies greatly across plans. Nine have assets with a market value less than 50 percent of their liabilities, 62 plans have less than 70 percent of liabilities and 81 plans have assets less than 80 percent."*

Moving on to even scarier stuff ...

The Great American mortgage & credit crisis

There is so much that could be said here to fill entire volumes for decades. However I just want to reference it to illustrate my point about the uncertainty of our times and the need for you to take personal responsibility for your own financial future.

For those of you that have attended my seminars and workshops in the past know that I was warning American homeowners about the looming housing market catastrophe since 2005. Those that heeded my advice to protect their homes escaped the tsunami of foreclosures that has devastated the lives of millions of families.

As a direct result of the "credit crunch" we have seen seemingly invincible Wall Street Goliaths like Bear Stearns and Lehman Brothers disappear overnight. In terms of the effect this fiscal crisis has had on personal wealth, the Federal Reserve reported (June 2012) that the median net worth of families plunged by 39 percent in three years, from $126,400 in 2007 to $77,300 in 2010. That put Americans roughly on par with where they were in 1992.

In September 2013, the Census Bureau reported that 2012 median household income was essentially stagnant at $51,017. Adjusted for inflation, that left income 8.3% lower than where it stood in 2007 before the recession. The poverty rate was 15%, with 46.5 million of our fellow citizens living at or below the official poverty line. That's 2.5% points higher than in 2007 and close to a post-War on Poverty record. Of this, 43% were in "deep poverty," with half below the poverty line. In 2000, the rate of poverty was 11.3%. In the late 1950s, before LBJ's War on Poverty began, the rate was above 22%.

No such thing as "Job Security"

If you think things are going to suddenly and magically improve, then you need to ... think again!

The latest polls indicate there is little, if any, relief on the horizon with ... 4 out of 5 U.S. adults struggling with joblessness, near-poverty or reliance on welfare for at least parts of their lives, a sign of deteriorating economic security and an elusive American dream. Survey data exclusive to The Associated Press pointed to an increasingly globalized U.S. economy, the widening gap between rich and poor, and the loss of good-paying manufacturing jobs as reasons for the trend.

Erik Brynjolfsson is a professor at the MIT Sloan School of Management. In June 2013, the MIT Technology Review reported that Brynjolfsson and his collaborator and co-author Andrew McAfee categorically proved that;

" ... impressive advances in computer technology - from improved industrial robotics to automated translation services - are largely behind the sluggish employment growth of the last 10 to 15 years. Even more ominous for workers, the MIT academics foresee dismal prospects for many types of jobs as these powerful new technologies are increasingly adopted not only in manufacturing, clerical, and retail work but in professions such as law, financial services, education, and medicine."

So you think your money's safe in the bank?

As I write this latest edition I remember another alarming economic headline that screamed; *"Bair Says Insurance Fund Could Be Insolvent This Year."* The article went on to say that Sheila Bair, Chairman of the Federal Deposit Insurance Corporation (FDIC), the fund used to protect consumer deposits at U.S. banks, was forced to defend new fees imposed on banks amidst an overwhelming outcry from the industry. Her reasoning is/was that without the new fees the fund could dry up thanks to the latest surge of bank failures. Could the FDIC become extinct putting all our savings at risk?

Ans: Everyone thought Lehman Brothers & Bear Stearns would be around forever too!

Meanwhile, for better or for worse, we now live in an interconnected and interdependent world whereby any number of unforeseen events from terrorism to a flu epidemic could completely derail the U.S. and global economies.

What does all this have to do with you Owning Your Home Years Sooner?

Ans: we now live in extremely uncertain economic times and the future is looking pretty grim. What you can be absolutely certain about is that you cannot rely on the corporate sector or the government to bail you out or to look after your financial future. Which means you have to take control of your own financial destiny. If you don't, you're going to end up joining tens of millions of newly impoverished Americans eking out an existence on food stamps and collecting roadside aluminum cans to buy dog food for your next meal.

Please, please, whatever you do, do not make the dire mistake of ever thinking that, *"That will never happen to me"* because your luck could change in an instant.

If it's any consolation, don't feel bad thinking you're the only one that's ill prepared. PwC's Financial Wellness Survey tracks the financial and retirement well being of working American adults nationwide. Their April 2011 survey uncovered that almost everyone is having problems making ends meet regardless of their income bracket. They revealed that almost half (49%) of working American adults found it difficult to meet their household expenses on time (up from 43% in 2010), and even those earning $100,000 or more annually said it's a challenge (36%).

The sun still shines above the clouds

My intent here is not to engage in fear mongering but to outline some harsh realities about the state of fiscal affairs in our country.

What I can also tell you is that despite the economic doom and gloom that may or may not happen, there is ALWAYS HOPE ... "IF" you choose to start developing the right mindset TODAY.

However, I also understand that you may feel somewhat overwhelmed by what you've just read. Furthermore, you may even feel a sense of powerlessness and therefore paralyzed into not taking any action at all. In which case – DON'T WORRY because a vast majority of people I share this information with have a similar reaction. They know that they need to do something to take care of their own financial future ...

The million-dollar question is, "where to start?"

My answer: you are already taking the RIGHT ACTION, RIGHT NOW by the mere fact you are reading this book.

Your immediate goal will be to use the Speed Equity® Mortgage Acceleration System to Own Your Home Years Sooner and at the very least Retire Debt Free. But you must begin that process today because every day that you don't apply this knowledge is another day you are sowing the seeds of your own financial demise.

Last, if this information comes as a surprise to you, then I urge you to pass this book on to as many people as possible because they most likely don't know it either.

Now, before I help you start your personal journey to financial freedom, there is an issue we have to address. And that is, developing the right mindset to Own Your Home Years Sooner & Retiring Debt Free. I will elaborate in the next chapter.

"Tomorrow is the most important thing in Life.
It comes unto us at midnight very clean. It's perfect when it
arrives and it puts itself in our hands. It hopes we've
learned something from yesterday."

- John Wayne -

Chapter 2
Exposing The Four Worst Money Myths

"It isn't what we know that gets in trouble,
it's what we know that ain't so."

- David Stockman -

Let your journey begin

I'm sure you've heard of the age-old adage: *"The journey of a 1,000 miles begins with the first step."*

And the journey I want you to take begins with you Owning Your Home Years Sooner and ends with you being financially independent ... and at the very least retiring debt free. The reason I want you to begin with paying off your home loan is because it's an aspect of finance that you are already familiar with.

If you have a mortgage (or are about to get one) then you already have a bothersome situation in your life. Therefore, I say let's begin there. I'm not going to ask you to learn a complicated investment strategy or be a financial genius. I'm simply going to teach you how to maximize the Return on Investment (ROI) of your existing financial resources to pay the least amount of interest on your mortgage ... and that's what the Speed Equity® Mortgage Acceleration System is all about. If you do this, you will rapidly build equity and increase your net worth. Once you master the basics of this System, you can then apply that very same knowledge and tools to begin and grow your investment portfolio that can support you in your retirement years.

In other words, what you are about to learn with this System will form an integral foundation to your long-term wealth creation. You can then decide whether you want to pursue more elaborate investment strategies once you have that foundational knowledge AND equity with which to invest. The best part is that once you grasp the idea of how easy it is to make your money work harder for you and develop the right fiscal habits for doing so, the art of making more money will really become fun.

BEWARE of "wealth creation" seminars

The first thing I want you to do right now is STOP and analyze what you think you have to do in order to become financially wealthy.

The reason I'm asking you to do this is because over the past 15-years I have attended and spoken at numerous "wealth creation" seminars and workshops where participants paid $1,000's to attend thinking they were going to learn something ... only to be pitched by other wealth creation gurus and seduced into spending $1,000's more to attend their seminars and workshops. What I am about to reveal has had me forever banished from this speaking circuit. But I believe that you deserve to be told the truth.

The dirty little INSIDER SECRET of the "wealth creation" seminar industry ...

... is a term called "funneling" ... and here's how it works ...

First you are invited to a "free" seminar - usually in the evening. This part is called a "lost-leader" because it's like bait to get you to attend. At this free seminar you never get any practical information - just little tidbits that you can't use unless you sign up for the weekend workshop. Here you have to pay but it's not an outrageous amount. At the weekend workshop you get some basic information and lots of anecdotes. However, the true agenda is getting you to sign up for the "mega" workshops. You're told that that's where you will meet true entrepreneurs that have "made it" with their program and subsequently, will discover the real insider secrets of the rich and shameless to make a fortune beyond your wildest dreams.

The ultimate goal of funneling is to whittle down the original audience to a core group. This is achieved through extremely high-pressure sales tactics and peer pressure to force attendees to sign up on the spot. Anyone that resists this indoctrination is directly and indirectly ridiculed as being some sort of failure and not truly serious about wanting financial success. In the end, most participants submit to the group's dynamics because they don't want to feel embarrassed or thinking that they are going to miss out on an opportunity of a lifetime. It's a lot like being forced into joining a doomsday cult.

Sadly, I have seen people in such groups lose all sense of reason and become fanatical about the seminar guru to the point they will do virtually anything they are told and turn into "seminar junkies". And once you are culled into this core group, you are robbed blind for all you're worth.

Without naming any names, in 2010, the Canadian Broadcasting Corporation (CBC) investigated seminars associated with one particular, world-renowned "get rich" author and guru on their consumer advocacy program, *Marketplace*. They found that one-day free seminars were conducted at which three-day courses were offered for $500. At the three-day classes, participants were offered longer courses priced between $12,000 and $45,000. A hidden camera was employed at a $500 seminar in Kitchener, Ontario, showing the trainer, advising participants to request that their credit-card limits be raised and giving out scripts with instructions on how to ask for limits as high as $100,000 to pay for the overpriced workshops.

Over the years this author's books and teachings have been criticized for focusing on anecdotes and containing little in the way of concrete advice on how readers should proceed. He responded by saying that his material is meant to be more of a "motivational tool" to get readers thinking about money rather than a step-by-step guide to wealth.

IMPORTANT CAVEAT: I want to be absolutely clear that I'm NOT at all suggesting that you should not pay someone for their service(s) especially if they bring tangible value to your table. What I am totally against is using the tactics I just described by the so called wealth creation industry to put you on an endless treadmill of seminars and workshops that cost $1,000's yet provide no real substance other than fluffy, feel-good rah-rah sessions.

Folks, there are plenty of similar retreats and seminars still being offered on the speaking circuit and I DO NOT ever want you to fall prey to this type of get-rich-quick pathway because it doesn't exist. I have personally seen good friends lose tens of $1,000's to these types of schemes and one particular story broke my heart.

Losing it all on the "wealth creation" seminar circuit

In 2004 I met a really lovely, hard working couple with two young kids aged three and five. Both husband and wife worked waiting tables at a small restaurant, and like most people, they just wanted a break to get ahead in life. They thought their luck had finally changed when they were invited by a friend to attend one of these "free" wealth creation seminars. Pretty soon, they got caught up in the groupthink hype of "you have to attend the next workshop if you're really serious" and lost everything. They ended up having to file for bankruptcy due to all the credit card debts they racked up to attend the next series of "must-do" workshops and also lost their home to foreclosure.

On a personal note, at one particular event where I was invited to teach about this System, I was pulled aside by the workshop organizer and told in no uncertain terms that what I was "selling" wasn't priced high enough. This well renowned seminar guru wanted me to come up with a makeshift workshop by the time I went on stage that evening and even told me how much I had to charge for it!!

Why?

Because he wanted half of what the workshop would cost.

I made it crystal clear for him, in no uncertain terms, what he could do with his workshop suggestion. At which point he threatened to remove me from his speaker list and I told him to "go ahead" because I went there to help people get out of debt - NOT to put them into more debt.

Anyway, I stood my ground and he relented. Needless to say, I was never invited back to speak at his workshops ever again or those of his cohorts ... even though I received no less than five standing ovations and 100% positive feedback on their post workshop presenter questionnaire.

If you feel as repulsed as I do about what really goes on in these so called wealth creation seminars, then please share these insider secrets with everyone you know so they don't get ripped off.

I warned you this was the *POLITICALLY INCORRECT, NO HOLDS BARRED, IN YOUR FACE, TELL IT LIKE IT IS EDITION.*

OK, so where to from here?

In this section I'm going to share with you some thought provoking insights based on research and personal observations over the past 25-years in helping people Own Their Homes Years Sooner. These lessons are in the form of myths people have around money. I need you to be aware of these myths if you want to succeed with the Speed Equity® Mortgage Acceleration System.

So here we go.

MYTH #1: Being "RICH" is the same as being "WEALTHY"

Let me give you the absolute best distinction I've ever come across between being RICH and being WEALTHY. I saw it in a comedy skit performed by Chris Rock.

Basically, he asks the audience; "What's the difference between rich and wealthy?" He goes on to say; " ... Shaq (O'Neil the NBA player) is rich. The (expletive) that signs his check is wealthy."

If you Google "The difference between rich and wealthy by Chris Rock" you can watch the entire clip on You Tube. It's absolutely hilarious. But the tragedy is that I've personally observed what he's describing, time and time again, regardless of age, ethnicity, gender or nationality.

What the Speed Equity® Mortgage Acceleration System does, and what I want for you, is to get you on the path to developing a "wealthy mindset" rather than being rich. It's a subtle distinction but once you "get it", it's like a skillset that you can apply over and over again to generate and manage your wealth.

At this stage I highly recommend you watch the clip by Chris Rock so we're on the same wavelength regarding this myth.

MYTH #2: Being "BROKE" is the same as being "POOR"

I've witnessed this particular phenomenon with a good friend I've labeled a "serial entrepreneur". This guy has been broke a number of times in his life with some of the ventures he's started. However, he always seems to bounce right up and make all his money back and then some. He currently owns one of the largest construction companies in the U.S. and despite the housing crisis, is one of the few builders actually making money. What I learned from my builder friend, and others like him is that being broke DOES NOT mean you are poor.

So what's the distinction here you ask?

I'll sum it up in one sentence ...

> Being broke is TEMPORARY, but being poor is usually a PERMANENT predicament.

You see it all comes back to that mindset of being wealthy. People with a wealthy mindset do go broke from time to time because not all their calculated business ventures pan out. However, they don't stay that way for very long. They quickly move on to their next enterprise, apply the lessons from all their previous ones and voila! They're back in the high life again.

How do they do this?

Ans: they've developed the mental aptitude of *how to make* money so they can apply this mindset over and over. Just to give you an idea of some very famous people that exemplify this temporary state of being broke, some going bankrupt several times in the process, include Walt Disney, Henry Ford, Donald Trump, George Foreman, and Francis Ford Coppola.

On the other hand, people with a "poor" mindset usually stay that way UNLESS they change. I'm not saying that poverty doesn't exist because it most certainly does. What I am talking about is a thing called a "poor" mindset or attitude. This worldview has a tendency of cementing people into a state of helplessness and powerlessness that keeps them in that predicament their entire lives.

So if you're broke right now, don't worry. Simply remind yourself that it's just a temporary situation ... as long as you don't have a poor mindset. What I can tell you is that what you will learn from applying the Speed Equity® System will not only help you pay off your home loan years sooner, but it will also help you start developing a mindset that will enable you to acquire long term wealth by using this System.

Myth #3: If I could just MAKE MORE MONEY

This is one of "the" most common statements I've heard people make over and over. It's based on the belief that their financial woes are due to lack of money. The funny thing is, people that make this statement never seem to have enough money regardless of how many pay increases they get, or how many extra jobs they work.

My best friend from high school summed it up in an astute observation one day as we were reminiscing about how little we needed financially to survive when we were at university ($7,500 per year), compared to the $18,000 annually we were earning in 1985 after our first year of graduation ... which in our opinion was making the "big-bucks" at that time. We noticed that the same people we knew that complained about lack of money when we were all at university were still complaining about the same thing years later when they were actually earning much more.

My friend remarked; *"You know Harj, it seems that these people's lifestyle somehow always rises up to meet their paycheck."*

That was such a profound statement that I remember it to this day almost 25-years later. How many people can you identify in your life that constantly complain about not having enough money and have always done so ever since you've known them? The biggest mistake that people make, for whom this statement is a daily mantra, is to believe that:

> **MAKING money is MORE important than MANAGING money**

Folks, knowing how to make money is important. However, managing what you have is even more vital.

Let me give you some factual research to help understand this. I'm sure you know that we as Americans are the world's largest consumers. Unfortunately, this has become such an epidemic in this country that we now have entire generations brought up to NOT manage money effectively and to live way beyond their means.

I already mentioned the 2011, Price, Waterhouse, Cooper study that revealed almost half (49%) of working American adults found it difficult to meet their household expenses on time, and <u>even those earning $100,000 or more annually</u> said it's a challenge (36%). Additionally, they found that nearly one-quarter (24%) of employees surveyed reported using credit cards to buy monthly necessities because they couldn't afford them otherwise. This was up nine percentage points from 2010, and among those earning $100,000 or more annually, that number jumped to 34%.

Now I can understand someone earning an "average" wage, with a family, having trouble making ends meet ... but those earning $100,000+ being in the same boat?! That to me is clearly a case of lifestyles rising up to meet a paycheck.

If you need more proof, let's go to the other extreme end of the income scale and look at pro athletes that earn millions of dollars. How could these people have financial problems you may ask?

Well, the March 29, 2009 issue of "Sports Illustrated Magazine" ran an article titled; "How (And Why) Athletes Go Broke". In it, they said, " ... athletes from the nation's three biggest and most profitable leagues—the NBA, NFL and Major League Baseball - are suffering from a financial pandemic." They went on, " ... although salaries have risen steadily during the last three decades, reports from a host of sources (athletes, players' associations, agents and financial advisers) indicate that:

- By the time they have been retired for two years, 78% of former NFL players have gone bankrupt or are under financial stress.

- Within five years of retirement, an estimated 60% of former NBA players are broke.

Remember, Dennis Rodman? He's a living example of this myth. Rodman played on the Chicago Bulls championship team with Michael Jordan and gained notoriety with his flamboyant antics on and off the court, including dating Madonna. Well, on March 27, 2012 the L.A. Times ran a story titled; **"Dennis Rodman 'broke,' ..."** The article went on to say that, "As of March 1, Rodman, 51, owed $808,935 in back child support ..." and faced 20 days in jail if he didn't pay it. At the time he filed for his third divorce in 2004, he listed his monthly expenses as more than $30,000!

What I really want for you to internalize here is that it is not enough to just have the ability to make money ... you have to know how to *manage it* as well. And that's exactly what the Speed Equity® System helps you to do.

MYTH 4: If I could just win the Lotto

How many times have you thought; "If I could just win the Lotto, all my troubles would be over?" Now be honest ... you know you've said this many times. Well, don't feel guilty because you're not alone in this thinking.

You see, a lot of people hold on to the unfounded belief that they will come into a sudden windfall and become "rich". In fact a 2005 study by the prestigious private bank Coutts and Co. (the bank the Queen of England uses) found that over 50% of people believe they may become a millionaire in their lifetime. Similarly, a 2003 Gallup poll found that 51% of Americans aged 18 to 29 thought it was "very" or "somewhat likely" that they would be rich one day. That number dropped to 8% for those 65 and over. Perhaps age does bring wisdom in the form of a reality check instead of a Lotto check. Sorry, Aussie humor at work here.

Unfortunately, even if you were to win the Lotto, history has proven time and again that winning a jackpot may just be the start of your woes both financially and emotionally. It all has to do with the previous three myths I just described.

Let me give you a case example ...

This is a story from my boyhood hometown in Perth, Western Australia and was featured in "The Sunday Times" on October 02, 2005. The headline read:

Lotto nightmare: relatives clean out dole duo's fortune.

By Paul Lampathakis (Oct. 02, 2005)

First of all, that headline immediately screamed to me; "what an oxy-moron".

I mean, how could winning the Lotto be a nightmare - right?

Unfortunately, it certainly was for this couple.

The gist of this financial disaster was that this welfare couple won no less than $793,151.87 in a Lotto jackpot. That's pretty close to a million dollars given that if you ever win any lottery prize in Australia, you DO NOT have to pay any taxes - AND - you get the entire jackpot in one lump sum.

Now take a guess at how long it took this welfare family to completely lose the entire amount? I'll give you a hint: 78% of NFL athletes go broke within two years of retirement and 60% of former NBA players do the same within five years.

In my opinion this couple set a world land speed record for blowing their money by doing it in seven (7) weeks. That works out to $113,307 a month ... beating Dennis Rodman by more than $83,000. The real tragedy was they continued to claim a total of $29,111 in welfare while they were burning through their cash, and consequently, were facing prosecution for defrauding the Commonwealth Government.

Right now, you're probably saying to yourself; "What the? ... How in the world could they screw this up so quickly?"

If we examine this story in terms of all four myths, it makes absolute sense.

Before I go on, I want you to Google, **"Lotto nightmare: Relatives clean out dole duo's fortune.** By Paul Lampathakis" and read what happened. I'd like to print the entire article here but out of respect for the paper's copyright terms, I cannot.

Once you've finished reading, we can dissect this story.

The synopsis I am about to give you is based on what I learned from a book called, **"The Success Syndrome"** by Dr. Steven Berglas. Dr. Berglas spent twenty-five years on the faculty of Harvard Medical School's Department of Psychiatry and is an expert on how people deal with success.

In his book, he describes in detail what happens to people that are ill prepared for success, financial or otherwise. His theory in terms of Lotto winners, or anyone else that comes into a sudden financial windfall and ends up losing it all, is based on a number of factors that work against them.

He said most "ordinary" people do not have the necessary financial or psychological acumen to deal with a large amount of money that is suddenly thrust onto them. Unlike business people, Lotto winners do not spend the time, and therefore do not have the opportunity to develop the necessary financial competencies that led them to acquire their fortune. This also means most of them lack the mindset to manage it themselves. This is evidenced by the fact that one of the first things they do is go on a spending spree and buy "stuff" that in most cases is not a good investment.

Next, they fall prey to all sorts of scoundrels disguised as financial advisors that are only too willing to take their newfound fortune off their hands. This is in contrast to business people, who in the process of building their wealth, also develop a whole host of contacts and networks over time to help them pick the right financial managers ... and carry out the necessary due diligence on them.

Finally, there is the psychological turmoil of winning a jackpot.

All of a sudden Lottery winners start receiving calls from long lost relatives, friends and complete strangers wanting a slice of the pie. This in turn makes them paranoid and question the motives of everyone around them. Last, they are thrust into an economic status that they are completely unprepared for and sometimes not entirely welcomed into because they didn't "earn it".

So there they are, unable to trust people from the past and not necessarily welcomed into their newfound socio-economic status. They feel isolated, confused, sometimes unworthy and the end result is a series of self-sabotaging behaviors that cost them their winnings and in most instances, leaves them destitute.

If we examine our case example of "the dole duo" in terms of the four myths ... we can see that these people were certainly NOT wealthy. They became rich very quickly as a result of their sudden windfall and acted out their lifestyle in accordance with that mental script (i.e. MYTH #1: Being "RICH" is the same as being "WEALTHY").

Sure they were broke. However, they also had a poor mindset. They did not have the skillset to create their wealth and in their attempt to be altruistic, they handed out money to please others who were also "poor" (MYTH #2: Being "BROKE" is the same as being "POOR"). The fact that they lost it all so quickly proves that no matter how much money they earn, they will most likely not acquire any long term assets (MYTH #3: If I could just MAKE MORE MONEY) - unless they change their mental attitudes and habits.

Finally, winning Lotto certainly did not bring good tidings for them (MYTH #4: If I could just win the Lotto). In fact, it's a sad ending to have one of your own relatives betray you to such an extent that you also face prosecution for welfare fraud.

As I said in the introduction, the Speed Equity® Mortgage Acceleration System is NOT a get-rich-quick scheme. It is a systematic, mathematically proven method to make your money work smarter. And if you are truly serious about building long-term wealth, this System will be an invaluable tool to help you achieve it.

In the next chapter, I'll outline the mindset you need to maximize your ROI using this System. I'm also going to share with you some hardcore research about millionaires that will absolutely blow your mind AND help you succeed with this System.

"Never stand begging for what you have the power to earn yourself."

- Miguel de Cervantes -

Chapter 3
The Right Stuff To Make The Speed Equity® System Work

"The willingness to do whatever it takes is infinitely more important than knowing everything there is to know about how to do it."

- Jamieson Squire Poignand -

If you want to save the maximum amount of time and interest using the Speed Equity® Mortgage Acceleration System, then here's what you must do ...

Step 1: Take Response-Ability

A lot of people think that in order to be wealthy you have to come from a wealthy background, or have lots of money to invest, or dress, or talk, or even act a certain way. Well, in all my years of helping people Own Their Homes Years Sooner, I observed that none of these things matter.

What I did notice however is that there is one fundamental difference between those who are wealthy, or eventually going to be wealthy, and those that are going to remain poor. And that fundamental difference lies in the way poor people and wealthy people approach life. Here's what I found ...

Poor people usually **make statements** about why they are poor. You may have heard some of these mantras yourself. Here's a sample of them; "The reason I don't have enough money is because ...

- I was born into poverty; or,
- My job doesn't pay me enough; or,
- I can't control my spending habits; or,
- I was never taught how to handle money, or,
- There just isn't enough to go around in the world; or,
- I'm too old to change my ways, or,
- I'm not smart enough/experienced enough to make money, or,
- The government/taxes always get me, etc. etc. etc.

Wealthy people (or those who will eventually become wealthy) usually **ask questions** about how to make money. They are always looking for opportunities and enquiring about how to increase their net worth. And once an opportunity presents itself, they then quickly take action on it.

You can see that one group **lays blame** for and **justifies** their financial plight, whilst the other group takes **responsibility** for their financial affairs. By making concrete statements about their financial predicament, poor people close the door to new opportunities. When they say, "I can't", it does not give opportunities a chance to be examined let alone actioned.

By asking the question, "How can I become wealthy?" you always keep open the door to new possibilities. And personally, I think anyone who is proactive in pursuing wealth, or happiness, or good health, or whatever they are passionate about deserves to get it. The best acronym I have ever heard that sums up what I mean about having such a mindset is ... **POOR** = "**P**assing **O**ver **O**pportunities **R**epeatedly."

Now before we go any further, I want you to examine that 'responsibility' word in a bit more detail because it is so vital to developing a wealth creation mindset. Unfortunately, most people see RESPONSIBILITY as a dirty 14 - letter word, a burden, and a cross to bear. Is it any wonder because the context in which it is most often used is to direct blame; "Who's responsible for this?"

Sound familiar?

In contrast, what I would like for you to do is develop a much healthier viewpoint about how you view the word responsibility, not from a negative standpoint but one of a positive and pro-active one.

You see, responsibility really means the ability to respond. It's the ability to choose your response. If we choose to take responsibility for our lives it means that we are 'RESPONSE-ABLE'. It's accepting that we are the creators of our own circumstances by choosing our responses to them. Which means that we can also change those circumstances if they are unsatisfactory.

So the first step in becoming financially free and developing a wealthy mindset is to stop laying blame and/or justifying why you don't have enough money and take the RESPONSE-ABILITY to make some. The mere fact that you are reading this book is testament to you taking Response-Ability to move on to greater things in your life.

Step 2: Know thyself

The second step to financial freedom is to become aware of your **money habits** and change them where necessary. Here's a very simple parable that best describes what a dysfunctional habit is and how to break it. It's called "The Story of Our Lives":

Chapter 1: I walk down a street and I fall into a hole. I'm frustrated, I'm angry and it takes me a while to climb out.

Chapter 2: I walk down the same street and I fall into the same hole again. This time I'm even angrier because I recognise that this is the same hole I fell into last time, and it takes me longer to climb out because of my increased frustration.

Chapter 3: I walk down the same street and I fall into the same hole again! This time I'm really riled, and I blame everyone for my predicament, and it takes me even longer to climb out.

Chapter 4: I walk down the same street and this time I see the hole, but I fall into it again! However, I keep my cool, I remember how to climb out and do so immediately.

Chapter 5: I walk down the same street, I see the hole and I also see a cover that's been lying next to the hole all along. I replace the cover and walk on.

Chapter 6: I walk down a different street.

Although simple, this little parable is very apt in helping us to examine what different groups of people habitually do with their money.

Recognizing what your most common money handling habits are will help to point out where you have been falling into the same holes. This awareness will also help you take response-ability to make the wealth creation journey safer and more prosperous by identifying what you need to do to change. I cannot emphasize how crucial a step this is in developing the right mindset for your wealth creation and using the Speed Equity® System to Own Your Home Years Sooner & Retiring Debt Free. Now let me share with you ...

The ultimate research data about wealthy people

At this point I'm going to highly recommend you get another book called; "**The Millionaire Next Door**" by Thomas J. Stanley and William S. Danko. The reason I want you to do this is because if you are truly serious about developing the proper mindset to becoming debt free and financially wealthy, then this is the book that will give you the complete inside scoop.

One of the reasons I love these authors is because they are hardcore academic researchers. Their book was first published in 1996, and in my opinion, is still "the" most comprehensive analysis of the timeless traits that millionaires have in common. So if you want to join their ranks, or at least be in a better financial position than where you are now, then what better way to do that than to learn the insider secrets from people that have actually done it - rather than seminar gurus, most of whom actually got rich by convincing you to attend their get-rich-quick workshops?

I'm not going to go into any detail here other than to mention just a couple of the traits the authors discovered that are also pertinent to making this System work for you. As I said, their book will help you understand the psychological and behavioral traits of a wealthy mindset and my System will get you started at a practical level to develop it.

What Stanley & Danko did was send out a 9-page "lifestyle questionnaire" with no less than 277 questions to people they identified as having a net worth of at least $1+ million. To their surprise they received 733 completed responses. Using these responses, they created a detailed profile of what a typical millionaire is and ... what they found absolutely blew them away!

You see, like most people, they thought millionaires lived flamboyant lifestyles in huge McMansions with servants and butlers, ate out at trendy restaurants, travelled the world in mega yachts, drove fancy cars, wore designer clothes, and showed off their bling at every opportunity. Incidentally, this is also the lifestyle that is heavily promoted by the so-called wealth creation seminar gurus because that's the TV fantasyland emotions they hook you in with using their funneling process. However, the reality according to Stanley & Danko was completely the opposite.

Their research concluded that the typical millionaire in their study shared seven (7) common traits that enabled them to successfully build and manage their wealth.

Here are four of the seven traits millionaires have in common:

1. **They LIVE WELL BELOW THEIR MEANS.** In general, millionaires are frugal. Not only do they self-identify as frugal, they actually live the life. They take extraordinary steps to save money. They **DON'T live lavish lifestyles**. However, they're willing to pay for quality, but NOT for image.

2. **They ALLOCATE THEIR TIME, ENERGY, AND MONEY EFFICIENTLY, in ways conducive to building wealth.** Millionaires budget. They also plan their investments. They begin earning and investing early in life. The authors also note that, "there is an inverse relationship between the time spent purchasing luxury items such as cars and clothes and the time spent planning one's financial future". In other words, the more time someone spends buying things that make them look good, the less time they spend on personal finance.

3. **They believe that FINANCIAL INDEPENDENCE IS MORE IMPORTANT than displaying high social status.** The authors found millionaires DON'T have fancy cars and DON'T buy top of the range designer clothes. They drive mundane domestic models that they keep for years and buy quality clothes off the rack.

4. **They are proficient at targeting opportunities and QUICKLY TAKE ACTION** rather than waiting for the perfect deal.

I can categorically tell you that if you apply my System, in the way that I have laid it out, it will fulfill the criteria of every single one of the abovementioned traits. You may not end up being a millionaire, but by golly, you're sure going to be in a much better financial position than where you are right now.

From infomercials to property tycoon

Let me conclude this chapter by sharing with you one of the best examples of someone that came from humble beginnings, chose to take response-ability, and became wealthy. I'll refer to him as Frank.

I met Frank at a seminar I was invited to present on this System by a local bank manager. I know what you're thinking, "greedy, no good bankers - right?" ... but there are people out there working in corporate institutions that truly care about their clients and this bank manager was one of them.

Anyway, Frank was very unassuming. He didn't stand out from the crowd and in fact looked just like every other audience member. At the end of my presentation, he came up to me and asked if I'd be willing to answer some questions about the Speed Equity® System in private. So, he invited me for a cruise on his yacht but I agreed to meet him over cup of coffee ... which he offered to buy.

I must confess that my initial reaction was, "The guy's got to be kidding. He has a yacht and he's sitting in a seminar on How To Own Your Home Years Sooner?" Nevertheless, I decided to play along and showed up at the designated Starbucks for my free coffee.

What he told me that day had me absolutely spellbound.

Frank said he fully owned no less than fourteen (14) rental properties that were generating him a residual monthly NET PROFIT of over $7,000. His net worth was over $2 million dollars and what he wanted to know was how to use my System to buy more investment properties.

That's not the part that floored me.

As we continued the conversation, I asked him what was his secret to becoming a multi-millionaire property mogul?

His reply ... "infomercials!!"

But, here's the catch ... he NEVER spent a penny to buy any of the late night programs he watched.

He said; "Harj I was just an average Joe with insomnia, with an average job, just wanting to get ahead in life."

He went on; "I started watching infomercials on how to buy investment properties but I didn't have the money to purchase any of the programs they were selling. But I was determined to make it."

"I decided if these people can do it, then so can I. So every day after work, I did research on the internet, bought a couple of books from Amazon and asked a lot of questions on chat forums. Next thing I knew, I'm at the local courthouse buying my first investment property. That was kind of scary, but after the next two, it became easier. I did make a couple of blunders that cost me money but I made sure I learned from my mistakes."

It took him over five years to get where he was financially and now, he spends his time just picking up "bargain" properties here and there and cruising on his yacht - which by the way he didn't recommend anyone purchase unless they're a boating fanatic like he is because he said; "Owning a boat is like standing at the edge of a fire pit and throwing in $100 bills."

As you can see, Frank embodied every single one of the Millionaire traits discovered by Stanley and Danko. His goal wasn't to take over the world. He just wanted to get ahead in life, provide for his family and spend time doing what he loved ... and he didn't spend $1,000's going to B.S. wealth creation seminars and workshops to do it.

The most humbling part for me was here's this guy, who's completely financially independent, and he made the effort to learn something new. He said to me; "Harj if I'd known about your System, I probably would have owned my properties a lot sooner." Over the years, I lost touch with Frank, but if by chance you're reading this book Frank, give me a call and let's catch up.

You can do it too!

My intent with the last two chapters wasn't to provide a long thesis on the psychology of building wealth but to point out some of the more common mental attributes required to develop a wealthy mindset and to succeed with this System.

I said it before and I'll say it again, I'm not promising that you're going to be a millionaire by using my System, but you're certainly going to be in a much better financial position if you do. I also want you to know that there is no magic formula that wealthy people have that enabled them to create their fortunes. In fact, the most common traits they share have been identified and documented in a highly respectable academic study ... and you can develop them too.

Finally, I have spent time outlining these attributes because from my personal experience in working with thousands of people, I can categorically tell you that I can give you all the knowledge, tools, and resources in the world to help you Own Your Home Years Sooner & Retire Debt Free, but unless you have the right mindset, it's never going to work for you.

What I can also tell you is that the Speed Equity® Mortgage Acceleration System will help you apply and develop every single one of the millionaire traits I mentioned using a very precise formula I call the "S.M.A.R.T." way to Owning Your Home Years Sooner & Retiring Debt Free.

So hang on to your hats because it's now time to introduce you to the Speed Equity® Mortgage Acceleration System.

> *"There are three types of people in the world:*
> *Those who MAKE things happen,*
> *Those who WATCH things happen, and*
> *Those who WONDER what happened."*

> - Dan Kennedy -

Introducing The Speed Equity® Mortgage Acceleration System

*"The significant problems we face cannot be solved at the same
level of thinking we were at when we created them."*

- Albert Einstein -

I want to begin this chapter by reassuring you that in order to use the Speed
Equity® Mortgage Acceleration System to Own Your Home Years Sooner &
Retire Debt Free - AND - save tens to hundreds of $1,000's in interest:

1. **YOU DON'T have to be a financial genius.**
2. **YOU DON'T have to Replace Your Mortgage to make it work, and ...**
3. **The Speed Equity® System is NOT MAGIC ... it's just MATH!**

The above three points are perhaps the most important I want to communicate
to you because there are plenty of unscrupulous people out there willing to
take your hard earned money by complicating this concept. My sole mission
when creating this System was to **EDUCATE and EMPOWER** homeowners like you to
get out of debt - NOT to put you into more debt.

For the remainder of this book I will teach you about the fundamental Key
Banking Principle I discovered way back in 1995. You will learn the SECRET
as to why a traditional mortgage takes so long to pay off. More importantly, I
will show you how to take full mathematical advantage of the Key Banking
Principle that lenders don't want you to know to Own Your Home Years
Sooner and save tens to hundreds of $1,000's in interest on your mortgage.

Incidentally ...

I want you to be a "Skeptic" but NOT a "Cynic"

What's the difference you may ask?

A skeptic is someone that has an open mind and asks a lot of questions
because they want to understand something. In fact, I love skeptics because I
proudly proclaim myself as one. However, I will tell you that I can't stand
cynics. Why? Because cynics are closed-minded and have already formed an
opinion. And no matter how much factual data you present to them, they will
not budge from their stubborn point of view. I'm sure you know a few of
those. With these types of people, I abide by the adage: **"Argue with a fool and then
you have two fools."**

Case in point, I get emails from readers saying; *"Have you read this blog?"*
Or, *"Did you see the comment so and so wrote about you on their website?"*
My answer is usually a flat, "No". I'm not trying to be dismissive, but I have
discovered that a lot of people out there dishing dirt on this concept have never
actually read my book or looked into the math behind this concept. They

simply like to have an opinion and are very eager to display it for their own narcissistic attention getting agendas.

My personal belief is that if you try and have an intellectual discussion with someone that has not done sufficient research on a topic, yet wants to argue for their opinion, is simply a pointless egotistical exercise and a waste of your time and energy. Therefore, I fully invite your skepticism about this concept but not your cynicism. What's more, I want you to ask a million and one questions until you "get-it". For example, I received the following response from one reader:

"I borrowed your book from a colleague at work, got inspired and then tried to explain your System to my wife.

"You were right. At first, she was very skeptical and thought it too good to be true. But after trying for several months to explain it to her, I simply got my own copy and said, "Just read this."

"The result led to both of us racing out the door to take action ... and now, we are well on our way to owning our home a lot sooner than we had dreamt possible!"

On that note, here are the ...

Three simple steps in the Speed Equity® Mortgage Acceleration System

First Step: is to read this book from cover to cover as you are doing. The greater you build your knowledge base, the more sophisticated your strategies will become in applying this System to save the maximum amount of time & interest on your mortgage.

Second Step: Having a personalized Speed Equity® Plan is critical if you want to achieve success with this System. You will learn how to do that without Replacing Your Mortgage and exposing it to the variable interest rate.

Third Step: This is the final step in applying the Speed Equity® System. Here I will guide you in getting the best loan to use with this System to bring the entire concept to life WITHOUT spending any money or having to refinance your existing one.

As you read on, you will see how each of these steps fit in the sequence, and why. Incidentally ...

The reason I call my Speed Equity® Mortgage Acceleration System a "System" as opposed to a program ...

Is because it has a very distinct and defined process to help you succeed, just like McDonald's® has a system to make their famous Big Mac® burgers.

Case in point: McDonald's® has a very rigid process to make a Big Mac®. They have a detailed manual instructing their employees about the exact ingredients they must have, how to prepare, cook, and assemble those ingredients in order to create a Big Mac®.

Consequently, if you order a McDonald's® Big Mac® in Sydney Australia or in Seattle, WA, you can rest assured that a Big Mac® will taste like a Big Mac® because it's created using a well-defined system.

In the same way, I have structured my Speed Equity® Mortgage Acceleration System and this book to make it extremely easy for you to understand and even easier to apply. I created it from the beginning to be a do-it-yourself system rather than trying to funnel people into exorbitantly priced seminars and workshops as I described earlier. The best way I explain to people as to why they should make the effort to understand this System is to say; "Imagine you're getting paid $100,000 cash just to spend one weekend to understand this concept. That's because for most people, that's the average amount of interest they save using it."

All I ask of you to do get on your way to accelerated home ownership is to make a commitment that you will follow the steps as I have outlined. And please, please, DO NOT try to short cut this System by skipping a step - unless you want to fail.

If you follow my instructions precisely, I am absolutely certain that once you start using it, you will be surprised at just how quickly you will start achieving RESULTS - and that is my definition of success. As far as I am concerned everything else is just hype.

To do this I will use some simple calculations and figures from real life case studies encountered during my early consulting and coaching days. You may note that some of the loan amounts in the examples will seem rather paltry and the incomes and expenses of the people concerned certainly do not put them in the mega-rich category. I have purposely selected these case examples to point out that my System is designed for ordinary people that have been using it since 1995.

For example, Nick and Christine, a couple that started using this System in February 1995. By August 2000, they completely owned their home and saved over $97,000 in interest. In that time, they were also well on their way to owning a third investment property. You can watch the original 1997 interview of this couple sharing their experience about the System on a

National Current Affairs TV Program and a follow up one in August 2000. It's archived on my website www.SpeedEquity.com

Last, in each chapter, I am going to build on your knowledge from the previous chapter. Some of you will get the concept very quickly and think that I am repeating myself. However, I want you to know that I have deliberately done this to ensure that everyone understands this System and I guarantee that you will learn something new by reading on. Besides, don't you think you owe it to yourself to learn as much as you can to save the maximum amount of time and interest on your mortgage?

Now let's get you started because ...

> *"A mortgage casts a shadow on the sunniest fields."*
>
> - R.G. Ingersoll -

Step 1: Chapter 5
The Great American Mortgage Tax Deductibility Scam

"An educated person is one who has learned that information almost always turns out to be at best incomplete and very often false, misleading, fictitious, mendacious - just dead wrong."

- Russell Baker -

In this chapter, we need to dispel one of the greatest lies that has been perpetrated and perpetuated on almost every homeowner in this country that keeps them enslaved to a 30-year mortgage. And that is, the belief that having a mortgage is actually "financially beneficial" for you. The reason, you are told this is because you can claim the interest on your mortgage as a tax deduction. As you are about to discover, nothing could be further from the truth. By the way, this is the only country in the world where you are allowed to claim your mortgage interest on an owner-occupied property as a tax deduction.

Here, I am going to address what I call "The Great American Mortgage Tax Deductibility Scam" that millions of homeowners just like you have been led to believe. This fallacy ends up costing you tens of thousands of dollars in unnecessary payments toward your mortgage that you can easily avoid. In fact, what you are about to read will shock you and may even make you angry.

Quite frankly, you have every right to be upset because you are about to learn that some of the very people you trusted to give you sound financial advice have actually misled you. That's because they didn't carry out sufficient research on this subject themselves. Many of them simply espouse the ignorance that was fed to them without having taken the time to investigate the facts. I sincerely hope you take this opportunity to realize the truth for yourself rather than relying on people that have a vested interest in keeping you chained to your mortgage for an entire lifetime.

The greatest con

Given half the chance, most people would love to pay off their mortgage.

However, they feel that that prospect is so far off in the distant future that they need some sort of compromise in the meanwhile. Consequently, a lot of people end up saying, *"I'm not paying off my mortgage because I want to use the interest as a tax write off."*

The assumption they're making when they say this is that because they can claim the interest on their mortgage as a tax deduction and minimize what they pay the IRS, that it must automatically mean they will have more disposable income. After all how many people do you know who believe that the less taxes you pay, the more money you'll have?

When it comes to your mortgage, this has got to be one of the biggest lies fed to keep an entire population in bondage to the single largest debt of their lives. The end result of this thinking is that it actually costs homeowners like you tens of thousands, if not hundreds of $1,000's, in extra interest on your mortgage because of your reluctance in wanting to pay it off sooner.

Unfortunately, not only educated homeowners but many financial advisors, tax specialists, accountants, lenders, bankers, real estate agents and mortgage brokers also blindly espouse this myth without actually having done the math. Sadly, in most of my seminars I have had seasoned bankers with decades of experience come up to me and say, *"Oh no, I never knew this and I've been telling my customers this fallacy for years because that's what I was told."*

As your advocate for accelerated home ownership I feel that it is my duty to set the record straight on this subject because as I said, it costs innocent homeowners like you tens of thousands of dollars in disposable income and keeps you subservient to your mortgage for much longer than is necessary. Therefore, in this chapter I am going to demonstrate that having a mortgage for which you can claim interest does reduce your taxable income. However, it DOES NOT benefit you financially in terms of disposable income.

The numbers never lie

First, using data from the Tax Rate Schedule in the IRS-1040 booklet, I'm going to create a hypothetical case example of two households filing their tax returns.

Furthermore, we are going to assume that the financial circumstances for both households are identical except that Household B has a mortgage and Household A does not because they decided to pay it off. Now, let's have a look at the TAXABLE and DISPOSABLE incomes each household has before and after taxes. Pay close attention to the figures in the table below.

	Household A	Household B
Gross Income	$65,000	$65,000
Mortgage	No	Yes
Interest on mortgage	$0	$11,567
Taxable income	$65,000	$53,433
Total Tax Paid	$13,896	$10,773
Difference in Tax Paid	+3,123	
Disposable Income	$51,104	$42,660
Monetary Advantage	+$8,444	

Table 1: Monetary Advantage of NOT Having a Mortgage

IMPORTANT: before I explain these results, I need for you to understand the distinction between TAXABLE and DISPOSABLE income.

Taxable income is the amount you pay taxes on AFTER all the deductions have been taken out. **Disposable income** is what you actually have in your pocket AFTER all taxes AND deductions have been taken out. So when it comes to spending power it's disposable income that's more important. I also want you to know that I am being extremely conservative in my calculations because I am NOT including the IRS Standard Allowable Deductions. Now based on these assumptions ...

As you can see from the table on the previous page, both households earn a gross income of $65,000 except Household B has a mortgage and Household A does not. Remember the assumption here is that Household A has paid off their mortgage.

You can also see that Household B paid $11,567 in mortgage interest to their lender. Consequently, Household B reduced their taxable income down to $53,433 and paid a total of $10,773 in taxes - according to the Tax Rate Schedule in the IRS-1040 booklet. Meanwhile, Household A did not have any mortgage interest to claim as a deduction and consequently paid tax on the entire gross amount of $65,000. As a result, the total tax paid here was $13,896.

At this stage everything is as it should be. That is, Household A does not have a mortgage on which to claim any interest and consequently has to pay tax on the entire gross income amount of $65,000. The end result is that Household A paid $3,123 more in taxes (i.e., Tax Paid Household A $13,896 - Tax Paid Household B $10,773 = $3,123).

However, here's where it all starts to go awry.

Take a look at the Disposable Income for each household.

Can you see that Household A, which has paid off their mortgage, has $8,444 more in disposable income (i.e., $51,104 - $42,660) than Household B even though they paid an extra $3,123 in taxes?

These results seem to go against everything that most homeowners have been told their entire lives. And that is, don't pay down your mortgage because you'll lose the tax write off, and presumably, will have less disposable income. However, through simple calculations we have revealed that this assumption is clearly false. Yes, having a mortgage will reduce your taxable income, but it DOES NOT mean you will have more disposable income.

How can this contradiction exist you may ask?

The logic is undeniable

For every dollar that Household B paid to the bank in interest on their mortgage, they got to claim 27 cents back as a tax deduction.

In contrast, Household A, which didn't have a mortgage and didn't have any interest to claim as a deduction (because they paid off their mortgage), kept the $11,567 as part of their taxable income. They then paid 27 cents on the dollar on this amount to the government and kept the remaining 73 cents as part of their disposable income.

The end result is that they had $8,444 more to spend for the year than Household B.

A simpler way to look at this

Assuming you are in the same tax bracket as the two households in our example, another way to look at these results is to ask yourself this simple question. *"Does it make sense to keep a mortgage so that for every $1 in interest you pay your lender you get to claim 27 cents back as a tax deduction?"*

"Or, would you rather pay off your mortgage, keep that $1 as part of your taxable income and pay 27 cents in taxes to the government instead?"

If the former makes sense to you, then please send me all the dollars you have and I'll send you back 50 cents for every dollar - GUARANTEED.

So yes, you will pay more taxes by paying off your mortgage. However, you're also going to have more disposable income.

Look at your own situation

As an exercise, I want you to take out your own tax statements for the past year and do some simple calculations.

1. Look at the amount of interest you paid to your lender on your mortgage for the year.

2. Next, find out what tax bracket you are in.

3. Now ask yourself this question, *"If you had paid off your mortgage and kept all the money you paid in interest as part of your taxable income, what would have happened?"*

I dare say the answer is very simple. You would have paid tax on that money at your marginal rate and kept the rest as part of your disposable income instead of it going to your lender. If you did this, how much more money would you have had in your pocket to spend for the year?

Why hasn't this myth been exposed before?

To answer this question you have to follow the money trail and find out who has a vested interest in promoting this fallacy. You will find that a lot of so-called "professionals" prefer to keep themselves - AND - their clients ignorant rather than digging out all the facts because they make money off of the status quo. For example, uninformed mortgage brokers, lenders, and bankers feed you this assumption to sell you bigger loans by telling you that you can claim the interest as a tax write off. Uninformed real estate agents do the same so they can sell you a bigger house. Most of these "professionals" are so convinced that a tax write off is the Holy Grail everyone should be chasing that they utterly fail to ask the question, *"Will a tax deduction on a mortgage lead to more disposable income for my clients?"*

For the average homeowner, the answer is clearly "NO."

As you can see, entire industries gain by making you think you should get the biggest mortgage possible and keep it for as long as possible. Those that are ignorant simply pass on their lack of knowledge. Those that know the truth, and are unethical, only give you half the truth so you think there is a financial gain to be had by keeping your mortgage. In the end, it is you who ends up paying tens of thousands of dollars in mortgage interest by holding on to it for so long.

Final exercise

Just to find out how many "advisors" around you have not taken the time to ask the right questions, I recommend that you call your CPA, real estate agent, banker, financial advisor and anyone else that has given you advice regarding the tax deductibility of your mortgage interest and ask them, *"Is it financially beneficial for me to pay off my mortgage or to keep it?"*

If they know what they are talking about, they should say something like this, *"Yes, having a mortgage on which you can claim the interest as a tax deduction will definitely reduce your taxable income. However, that doesn't necessarily mean that you will have more disposable income."* If they say anything contrary to that, I recommend you tell them to get a copy of this book and read this chapter. After reading it ...

They will either have to admit that they deliberately lied to you or show their incompetence by not having examined all the facts and passing on ill advice. Remember the bottom line is, does it make sense to pay out $1 in interest on your mortgage so you can claim 27 cents back as a deduction? Or would you rather pay off your mortgage and keep that $1 as part of your taxable income?

By the way, I'm not saying that you should discount how you structure your personal finances and investments to maximize your tax benefits. However, thinking that you're moving ahead financially by keeping your mortgage just doesn't make any sense because the only one benefiting from this is your lender and all the hangers on.

Incidentally, has your lender made the effort to tell you the full story about this subject lately? In fact, go to any lending institution's website and you will see that all they talk about is the tax deductibility aspect and nothing more because they are the ones gaining off of your lack of knowledge.

When does it make sense to get a mortgage?

Short answer: if you're renting.

Having said that ... it depends on a number of pros and cons. I won't go into detail but keeping to this chapter's theme of the tax deductibility on mortgage interest, a strong argument can be made for getting a mortgage to buy a home vs. renting. That's because now, the interest on your mortgage becomes tax deductible whereas a rent payment is not ... there are some exceptions to this rule such as when you run a home business. Furthermore, when all is said and done, you will be building equity in your own home and have something to show for your monthly payments rather than helping someone else become wealthy.

Of course the benefits of homeownership need to be carefully weighed against the cons such as responsibility for maintenance, taxes, mortgage payments, lack of mobility, etc. You should pay close attention to that last point because if you plan on moving, then it may NOT make sense for you to buy a home as you could end up losing money when trying to resell it. That's especially the case if home values remain stagnant from the time you buy a home to when you sell it. In this scenario, you will most definitely lose money as you factor in the cost of selling your home (approx. 8%) AND paying loan origination fees to buy a new one.

In a nutshell, getting a mortgage to buy a home puts you in a better long-term financial position than renting "IF" you plan on staying in your home over an extended period of time. However, once you have a mortgage, you should pay it off as quickly as possible.

Final thoughts for your consideration

Remember in Chapter 1 ("Why You Should Own Your Home Years Sooner As An American") I referred to the 2003 report to Congress from the Board of Trustees of the US Social Security System? Three of the points they went on to make in that report were:

- "The projected point at which tax revenues will fall below program costs comes in 2018." (Of course we now know it's much earlier than that).

- "Today, there are 3.3 workers paying Social Security payroll taxes for every one person collecting Social Security benefits. That number will drop to 2-to-1 in less than 40-years. At this ratio there will not be enough workers to pay scheduled benefits at current tax rates."

- "As stated in the Trustees Report, the sooner we address the problem, the less abrupt the changes will have to be."

In my 2003 U.S. edition, I also outlined these facts and told readers to take particular note of the emboldened text. I then asked them to put themselves in the shoes of the policy makers for a moment and posed the question; *What options do you think you would have to exercise in order to take care of your ever-increasing number of retiring constituents?"*

The options I put forward were:

1. To INCREASE Medicare and Social Security tax rates to make up for the projected shortfall.

2. DECREASE the amount paid to Social Security recipients.

3. Either REDUCING OR COMPLETELY ABOLISHING the tax deductibility of interest on home loans and using that as an added revenue stream to fund these programs. I would now add a fourth ...

4. INCREASE the retirement age at which these benefits are paid.

Aren't our policy makers discussing these courses of action lately?

Think it won't happen?

If you look at history, you will find that desperate situations often lead bureaucrats to take desperate measures. And the Medicare and Social Security forecasts are one of those extremely desperate situations. So desperate in fact, that the solutions have gained bi-partisan support. Here is an article from the Seattle Times dated July 11, 2010, titled, "Will we lose mortgage deductions, Medicare?" and I quote ...

> "The chairmen of President Obama's national debt commission painted a gloomy picture Sunday as the United States struggles to control its spending.
>
> Republican Alan Simpson and Democrat Erskine Bowles told a meeting of the National Governors Association that everything needs to be considered including curtailing popular tax breaks, such as the home-mortgage deduction, and instituting a financial trigger mechanism for gaining Medicare coverage."

These forecasts are not hypothetical, my friends. They are facts that need to be taken very, very seriously by everyone. As I said earlier, rather than blaming others when it's too late, it is a most prudent person that takes control of their own destiny - NOW!

Having said that, imagine how different your thinking processes will be when you Own Your Home. In fact, why don't you take a moment to ponder that right now before I share with you how it all works in the next section?

"Education is learning what you didn't even know you didn't know."

- Daniel J. Boorstin -

Step 1: Chapter 6
How Banks Make Their Profits

"The meek shall inherit the Earth, but not its mineral rights."

- J. Paul Getty -

In order to Own Your Home Years Sooner and save tens to hundreds of $1,000's in interest, you have to understand three things:

1. The type of mortgage that lenders want you to apply for.

2. How lenders want you to service your mortgage.

3. Why lenders want you to do this?

1. The type of mortgage that lenders want you to apply for

The type of home loan most commonly offered by the lenders is referred to as a 'Principal & Interest (P&I) Loan'. That's because you are not only paying interest on the money you borrowed, but you are also reducing the 'Principal' (the amount borrowed) - albeit very, very, slooooooooowly. Next thing you have to know is ...

2. How lenders want you to service your mortgage

Not only are you told to take out a 30-year P&I loan, but you are also taught, encouraged, and brainwashed into managing your personal finances and servicing your mortgage as per the schematic below.

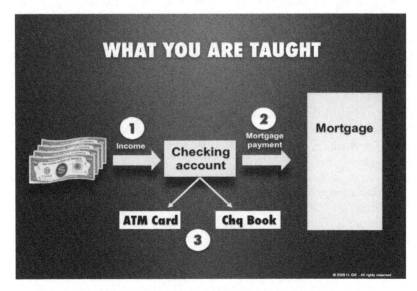

Fig. 1: What lenders teach, encourage & brainwash you to do.

Here's what's going on in Fig. 1:

1. You have a checking account into which you deposit your income.

2. Once a month you make your mortgage payments from your checking account using online banking or mailing a check to your lender.

3. What's left over in your checking account you draw out for living expenses using an ATM card or a checkbook?

Does this sound familiar to you?

Well, that's what everyone in the Western Industrialized world is taught, encouraged and brainwashed into doing in order to manage their personal finances and to service their mortgage.

3. Why do lenders want you to do this?

To answer this, you have to understand how banks make money and here's the insider SECRET ... first, they magically multiply your money using a principle called "Fractional Banking". Then, they use this funny money to make more money for themselves. Once you understand this, you will be in no doubt as to why lenders want you to service your mortgage in the way I just described and how you can use this knowledge to Own Your Home Years Sooner & Retire Debt Free.

By the way, what I'm revealing to you is readily available on the internet. In fact, if you logon to **WIKIPEDIA** and type the search term "Fractional Banking", here's what you will find, and I quote:

*"**Fractional-reserve banking** is the banking practice in which only a fraction of a bank's deposits are kept as reserves (cash and other highly liquid assets) available for withdrawal. The bank lends out some or most of the deposited funds, while still allowing all deposits to be withdrawn upon demand. Fractional reserve banking is practiced by all modern commercial banks!*

When cash is deposited with a bank, only a fraction is retained as reserves and the remainder can be loaned out (or spent by the bank to buy securities). The money lent or spent in this way is subsequently deposited with another bank, creating new deposits and enabling new lending. The lending, re-depositing and re-lending of funds expands the money supply (cash and demand deposits) of a country. Due to the prevalence of fractional reserve banking, the broad money supply of most countries is a multiple larger than the amount of base money created by the country's central bank.

***Banks make a profit based** on the difference between the interest they charge on the loans they make, and the interest they pay to their depositors."*

So there you have it folks. You now have a much better understanding of how the banking system operates than 99.9999% of the general population. On that note, have you ever noticed the huge difference between what lenders pay out on a typical checking account and what they charge for a typical 30-year P&I loan (see Fig. 2 below) ...

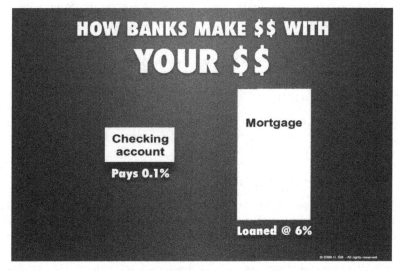

Fig. 2: How lenders make their money.

Looking at the above schematic, you don't have to be a rocket scientist to work out that there is a difference of 5.9% in the banks' favor (i.e. they pay you 0.1% in interest on your checking account and turn around and lend that money back out at 6% to home loan borrowers - much higher rates for personal and car loans).

 INSIDER SECRET

OK, so here it is ... the big INSIDER SECRET that lenders don't want you to know about AND the reason they hate the Speed Equity® Mortgage Acceleration System so much is because ... it completely *demolishes their ability to make a profit off of your money!*

It does this by bridging the gap between the interest they pay you on your checking/ savings account and what they charge for a mortgage. By using this System and the Key Banking Principle, you will learn how to completely reverse the lenders' profit making process - *in your favor!* This fact will become crystal clear as you read on.

"There are few nudities so objectionable as the naked truth."

- Agnes Repplier -

Step 1: Chapter 7
Your Prison Made From Pennies

"Compound interest is the eighth wonder of the world.
He who understands it, earns it ... he who doesn't ... pays it."

- Albert Einstein -

The Key Banking Principle

The interest on your mortgage is calculate on the DAILY OUTSTANDING BALANCE and charged at the end of the month (called monthly in arrears).

Now that you have a working knowledge of how the banking system operates and how lenders make their profits, it is time to start learning how to take full mathematical advantage of that information to Own Your Home Years Sooner & Retire Debt Free.

In the last chapter, I outlined for you the type of home loan most commonly offered by the banks, called a 'Principal & Interest (P&I) Loan'. I also exposed what you and almost every other home loan borrower around the world is taught, encouraged and brainwashed to do in order to enslave you to a typical P&I loan. What I can now reveal to you is that the whole SECRET to paying off your home or investment loan years sooner hinges on you understanding and taking full mathematical advantage of the abovementioned Key Banking Principle I discovered in 1995. In order to do that, we need to examine, in minute detail, why a typical P&I loan keeps you subjugated to it for 30-years. Let's do that through a simple illustration.

Case Example

LOAN AMOUNT:	$250,000
LOAN START:	Jan. 01, 20XX
INTEREST RATE:	6%
FREQUENCY OF PAYMENTS:	Monthly
LOAN TERM:	30 years
PAYMENT AMOUNT:	$1,498.88 per month

The above situation is very typical. A couple takes out a $250,000 home loan on Jan. 01, 20XX at 6% interest that is amortized over 30-years. Why did they do this? Because that's what everyone else does. And in order to service this loan, they would have to make monthly payments of $1,498.88 every single month for the next 30-years. Folks, just think about this for a moment ... people spend less time in prison for murder than it takes for you to throw off the shackles of your 30-year mortgage.

How interest is calculated

Keeping in mind our Key Banking Principle (i.e. interest is calculated on the daily outstanding balance of your mortgage and charged monthly in arrears). We note this couple started their P&I loan in January 20XX owing $250,000. And because they were making monthly payments, their Daily Balance remained at $250,000 for each day of January until they made their payment (on the last day of January). As I said, that's because lenders calculate the interest payable for a full month and then charge you that interest at the end of the month called **monthly in arrears**.

Here's what happens to this $250,000 mortgage ...

Based on the way this couple were forced to service their P&I loan, let's take a look at the Daily Balances of this $250,000 mortgage for the first four months.

Month	Daily Balance	Cumulative Payments	Cumulative Interest Paid	Cumulative Principal Reduction
Jan	$250,000.00	$1,498.88	$1,273.98	$224.91
Feb	$249,775.09	$2,997.76	$2,423.62	$574.14
Mar	$249,425.86	$4,496.64	$3,694.67	$801.97
Apr	$249,198.03	$5,995.52	$4,924.71	$1,070.81

Table 2: Daily Balances of $250,000 mortgage over first four months.

Remember, our couple took out their $250,000 mortgage on Jan. 01, 20XX.

Consequently, the Daily Balance for this loan stays at $250,000 for every single day of January until they make their first mortgage payment of $1,498.88 at the end of the month. They would find that a large chunk of their payment (i.e. $1,273.98) disappears on interest, leaving them with a paltry $224.91 reduction in the amount borrowed for the following month.

This then gives them a new Daily Balance for the month of February (i.e. $249,775.09) that stays the same for every single day of February, until they make their next mortgage payment at the end of the month. Now, they've paid their lender a total of $2,997.76 in payments of which $2,423.62 has disappeared on interest - leaving them with a $574.14 principal reduction for the total amount borrowed.

Same thing happens in March i.e. the Daily Balance reduces to $249,425.86 and stays the same for the entire month. The cumulative payments add up to $4,496.64 of which a total of $3,694.67 has been consumed by interest.

This cycle repeats itself month after month. They make their mortgage payment at the end of each month, a large chunk of that payment disappears on interest, leaving only a small portion to reduce the Daily Balance with for the following month. I am sure you're familiar with this cycle if you have a 30-year P&I loan. When we look at the line graph of the loan amount owed each year, it looks like this ...

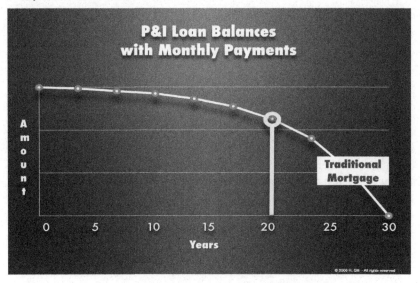

Fig. 3: Yearly P&I Loan Balances on 30-year mortgage.

When you examine Fig. 3 (above) more closely, you will notice that for the first twenty-two odd years, you hardly make a dent in the amount borrowed. The pure and simple reason for that is due to ...

> ### The Key Banking Principle
>
> The interest on your mortgage is calculate on the DAILY OUTSTANDING BALANCE and charged at the end of the month (called monthly in arrears).

As I said, because you are forced to service your loan by making monthly payments, the Daily Balance on your mortgage stays high and stays the same for the entire month until you make your next payment. Meaning, the interest accumulates for the entire month on the high monthly balance and when you make your payment, a large portion of it goes toward servicing the interest cost.

By the way, why is it that for the first twenty-two odd years your payments will hardly make a difference to the amount borrowed, and then all of a sudden it starts to reduce at a rapid rate?

Ans: Because mathematically that's just the way it works out.

You see, at the twenty-two year mark, you hit a mathematical critical mass whereby more of your payments start to go toward paying down the principal rather than being consumed by the interest. From that point forward, the loan amount reduces quite dramatically. In fact, it doesn't matter if your loan amount is for $100,000 or a $100 million. If you amortize it over 30-years, that's exactly what you will see in terms of yearly balances on a line graph - AND - it's all because of the Key Banking Principle.

How to spot ignorant people

There are a lot of people out there that have jumped on the mortgage acceleration bandwagon with their slapstick software programs trying to make a quick buck. Regrettably, most of them have absolutely no idea about how the banking system works and especially no idea about the Key Banking Principle. You can easily identify them because they try to make it sound as if there's some sort of gigantic banking conspiracy to keep you enslaved. They show their utter ignorance by making the following statement:

> "Lenders FRONT LOAD the interest on your mortgage.
> That's why it takes you so long to pay it off!"

If you hear anyone making the above statement, take heed and run the other way because they have absolutely no idea what they're talking about. In fact, you can actually enlighten them by saying:

"Listen dummy. Lenders don't "front-load" the interest at all. The reason it takes 30-years to pay off a traditional P&I loan is because the interest on that type of loan is calculated on the Daily Balance and charged monthly in arrears. And because you only affect the Daily Balance once a month and only by a very small amount each time, the Daily Balance of a P&I loan remains the same and remains high throughout the entire month. Consequently, more of your payments go toward servicing the interest on your P&I loan rather than reducing the amount owed until the twenty-two year mark. At that point the loan starts to reduce quite dramatically because more of your payments start going toward reducing the loan balance rather than being consumed by interest because it hits a mathematical critical mass point. It's NOT a conspiracy. It's NOT magic. Its just math."

I know it may sound somewhat harsh in the way I articulated that, but quite frankly, I've had enough of all the charlatans that try to take advantage of innocent homeowners like you by making it sound as if they have some sort of insider information about a banking conspiracy. Besides, I did pre warn you by saying this is the POLITICALLY INCORRECT, tell it like it is, in your face edition of my book. My job here is to educate you about knowledge that has been around for a very long time so you are empowered to take advantage of it. The only conspiracy here, if you want to call it that, is the banking industry's reluctance in sharing this information with you.

By the way, here's the formula lenders use to calculate the amount of Daily Interest charged:

Daily Interest = [Loan Amount x Interest Rate] / 365 days

The real SECRET that keeps you enslaved to a 30-year P&I loan

What I am about to show you is "the" most important set of figures in this entire book. I call it "Your Prison Made From Pennies." So here goes.

You now know what the Key Banking Principle is, in that the interest on your mortgage is calculated on the Daily Balance and charged monthly in arrears. You also know that the Daily Balance on your mortgage stays high and stays the same for the entire month until you make your next payment.

Let's now take a look at the Daily Interest charged on this $250,000 P&I loan for the first four months (see Table 3 below).

Month	Daily Balance	Daily Interest Charged	Difference in Daily Int. Charged
Jan	$250,000.00	$41.09	
Feb	$249,775.09	$41.06	- 3¢ per day
Mar	$249,425.86	$41.00	- 6¢ per day
Apr	$249,198.03	$40.96	- 4¢ per day

Table 3: Daily Interest Charged on $250,000 mortgage over first 4-months

As you can see, the Daily Balance for the month of January stays at $250,000. Consequently, the Daily Interest charged is $41.09 per day for each and every day of January. The couple then makes their monthly payment of $1,498.88 and the Daily Balance for February reduces to $249,775.09 and stays the same for each day of February. Consequently, the Daily Interest charged is now $41.06 per day. Folks, that's a ...

> . . . reduction in the Daily Interest Charged by a total of 3¢ per day from the previous month!

And when they make their monthly payment at the end of February, the Daily Balance for March drops down to $249,425.86. As a result, the Daily Interest charged also reduces by a whopping 6¢ per day from the previous month. Note: it has taken an entire two months to reduce the Daily Interest charged by a total of 9¢ per day.

Same thing happens in April. The Daily Balance is reduced and the Daily Interest charged also reduces ... by a further **4¢ per day** from the previous month!

By the way, why is there a difference in the Daily Interest charged for each month?

Ans: because not all months have the same number of days. So in order to calculate the interest that would be charged for each month, you would multiply the Daily Interest charged by the number of days in that month:

i.e. Monthly Interest = Daily Interest Charged x No. of Days in Month

Getting back to our case example, I know it doesn't sound very exciting does it? I mean a reduction in the Daily Interest charged by 3¢ per day, 6¢ per day and 4¢ per day doesn't make anyone want to run out onto the street shouting; *"Yeeeaaahhhh, I've reduced my Daily Interest charged by 4¢ per day this month."*

But you see, bankers and lenders know this because that is the power of **compound interest**. They know that most people will pay absolutely no interest (no pun intended) to these humble little pennies because they're just pennies. They rely on you ignoring this very obvious, unobvious fact. Couple this with the way you are forced to service your mortgage as I described, that only allows you to reduce the Daily Interest charged by pennies at a time, and here's what happens to a typical 30-year, $250,000 P&I loan ...

Year	Cumulative Payments	Amount Still Owed
5	$89,932.80	$232,142.63
10	$179,865.60	$208,055.22
15	$269,798.40	$175,563.19
20	**$359,759.20**	**$131,759.09**

Table 4: Principal Reduction on $250,000 mortgage over 20-years

As you can see, after twenty years of making monthly payments of $1,498.88 on this $250,000 P&I loan, the total payments would add up to $359,759.20 and you would still owe your lender more than half of the original principal amount (i.e. $131,759.09).

After 30-years, the total payments would add up to $539,596 on this $250,000 P&I loan because along the way, you would have also paid $289,596 in interest (see Fig. 4 on the next page). That's what happens when you are only allowed to reduce the Daily Interest charged by pennies at a time. Now do you see why I call it "Your Prison Made From Pennies" ... because it's all about the pennies?

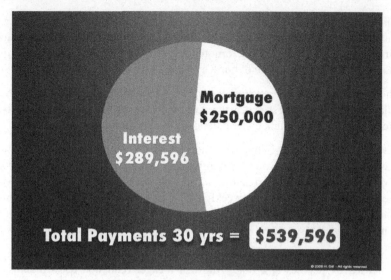

Fig. 4: Total payments on a 30-year, $250,000 P&I loan.

Another way to look at this ...

... Is to ask yourself the question, *"How many houses am I really being forced to pay for?"*

Ans: for a typical 30-year P&I loan, regardless of the loan amount is TWO (see Fig. 5 below). That makes one for you and one for the bank ... and that's just the way they like it!

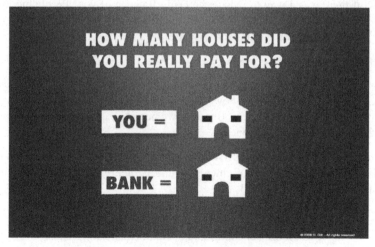

Fig. 5: Number of homes you pay for with a 30-year, P&I loan.

Phew, I bet you thought we'd never get through this chapter - huh?

I know some people start rolling their eyes and get brain fog when looking at the numbers in this chapter. However, we absolutely have to drill down to this level of detail with the calculations because the results are absolutely undeniable and therefore necessary in blowing away the smoke and confusion surrounding this concept. They form the very core to understanding and taking full mathematical advantage of our Key Banking Principle.

Therefore, thank you for sticking through this chapter because after all, we are talking about "the" most expensive purchase you are likely to make in your lifetime and ... I also think congratulations are in order for doing so.

To summarize, "the" most important point I wanted to emphasize in this chapter was that the interest on your P&I mortgage is calculated on the Daily Balance and charged monthly in arrears ... and if you are making periodic payments (i.e., monthly, bi-weekly, or, weekly), the Daily Balance of your P&I home loan stays high and stays the same for the entire month until the next payment is made.

When we looked closely at the Daily Interest charged, you noticed that it only decreased by pennies at a time. And that meager reduction takes months to achieve. However, over the term of your P&I loan, these pennies add up to hundreds of thousands of dollars in interest because of compound interest. That's the SECRET that bankers know and don't tell you about because on the surface it seems so insignificant. That's the real conspiracy. Therefore, most people ignore this fact and they want you to keep ignoring it because this keeps you enslaved to your P&I loan for almost half your adult life. In other words, it's all about the pennies and that's why I call this chapter; "Your Prison Made From Pennies."

Now, if there was a way to reduce the Daily Balance of your P&I home loan, then this would obviously reduce the amount of interest you would have to pay and also reduce the term of the loan, right?

Correct.

This will be explained in much more detail in the chapters to follow and this is precisely what I am going to show you how to do by using the Speed Equity® Mortgage Acceleration System. But first, we need to examine some traditional outdated methods of loan reduction.

Remember, the more you understand about how your mortgage is structured and works, the more time and interest you are going to save. I think the best quote to sum up this chapter is ...

"If you think something small cannot make a difference,
try going to sleep with a mosquito in the room."

- Ben Hurn -

Step 1: Chapter 8
Traditional Outdated Methods of Loan Reduction

"If the rhythm of the drum beat changes,
the dance step must adapt."

- West African proverb -

In the last chapter, we saw how and why using a traditional P&I loan with monthly payments takes 30-years to pay off. And that's all due to the Key Banking Principle and the way you are forced to service this type of mortgage. Consequently, over the first twenty-two years of a typical 30-year P&I loan, most of your payments go toward paying for the interest on the loan while only a small portion actually goes toward reducing the principal amount borrowed.

The table below shows the End of Year Balances for a $250,000 P&I home loan (with monthly repayments of $1,498.88) at an interest rate of 6%.

End Yr.	Total Payments	Principal Paid	Interest Paid	Mortgage Balance
1	$17,986.56	$3,070.06	$14,916.50	$246,929.94
2	$35,973.12	$6,329.48	$29,643.64	$243,670.52
3	$53,959.68	$9,789.95	$44,169.73	$240,210.05
5	$89,932.80	$17,364.34	$72,568.46	$232,635.66
10	$149,888.00	$40,786.24	$139,079.36	$209,213.76
15	$269,798.40	$72,378.89	$197,419.51	$177,621.11
20	$259,731.20	$114,992.63	$244,738.57	$135,007.37
25	$449,664.00	$172,472.15	$277,191.85	$77,527.85
30	**$539,596.80**	**$250,000.00**	**$289,593.34**	**$0.00**

Table 5: Amortization schedule for a 30-year, $250,000 P&I loan

After 15-years, a total of $269,798.40 worth of payments would have been made with only $72,378.89 of the principal being reduced. After 30-years the total amount of interest paid (i.e. $289,593.34) is more than the original $250,000 loan amount borrowed. If you have a 30-year P&I loan right now, then this is exactly what is happening to you regardless of the size of your loan amount.

The situation I have just described is not uncommon. What's more, many people think that there's not much they can do about accelerating the reduction of their P&I home loan other than engaging in one of the following outdated methods of accelerated loan reduction ...

Paying bi-weekly (also called "fortnightly" in some countries)

You probably know by now that paying bi-weekly rather than monthly will cut years off your home loan. The way it works is as follows ...

Example: Home loan of $250,000 at 6% interest amortized over 30-years with monthly payments of $1,498.88. This means that you will be making twelve equal sized payments of $1,498.88 each year.

i.e., $1,498.88 x 12-months = $17,986.56

However, if you choose to divide this monthly figure in half and pay fortnightly, this is the result:

$749.44 x 26 fortnightly payments = $19,485.44

If you compare the figures for the two repayment methods you get a difference of exactly $1,498.88.

i.e., $19,485.44 - $17,986.56 = $1,498.88 = 1 month's extra repayment.

So you can see that by dividing the original monthly repayment in half and paying this amount bi-weekly, you will actually make one extra month's payment per year (in this case an extra $1,498.88 per year). This will reduce the term of this P&I loan from 30-years down to 24-years and 6-months.

Therefore, servicing a P&I loan of $250,000 at 6% interest with bi-weekly payments of $749.44 would result in the following End of Year Balances:

End Year	Total Payments	Principal Paid	Interest Paid	Mortgage Balance
1	$19,485.44	$4,800.37	$15,434.46	$245,199.63
2	$38,970.88	$9,714.05	$30,006.17	$240,285.95
3	$58,456.32	$14,931.22	$44,274.39	$235,068.78
5	$97,427.20	$26,352.15	$71,824.25	$223,647.85
10	$194,854.40	$61,678.75	$133,924.61	$188,321.25
15	$292,281.16	$109,773.05	$184,006.70	$140,226.95
20	$389,708.80	$174,246.28	$216,960.44	$75,753.72
25	**$477,393.28**	**$250,000.00**	**$227,565.46**	**$0.00**

Table 6: Amortization schedule of $250,000 P&I loan with fortnightly pmts.

After 15-years, a total of $292,281.16 worth of repayments would have been made with $109,773.05 of the principal being paid off. This is $37,394.16

more in principal reduction when compared to our original monthly repayment method.

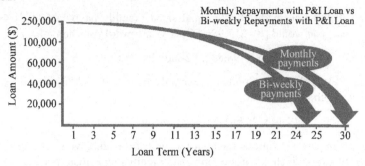

Fig 6: Monthly repayment vs. bi-weekly/fortnightly method.

Below is the end of year balance comparisons for both the monthly and the bi-weekly repayment methods:

End Year	Principal Owed (Monthly Payment)	Principal Owed (Bi-weekly Payment)
1	$246,929.94	$245,199.63
2	$243,670.52	$240,285.95
3	$240,210.05	$235,068.78
5	$232,635.66	$223,647.85
10	$209,213.76	$188,321.25
15	$177,621.11	$140,226.95
20	$135,007.37	$75,753.72
25	$77,527.85	$0.00

Table 7: Yearly loan balances monthly vs. bi-weekly payment methods

In effect, the bi-weekly repayment method would reduce our $250,000 loan at 6% interest from 30-years down to 24-years and 6-months and result in an interest saving of $62,027.88. Not a bad ROI wouldn't you say? But if you want to know how to Own Your Home Even Sooner, then keep reading because there is a much better way to do that by using the Speed Equity® Mortgage Acceleration System.

Paying weekly

Contrary to what some people may think, paying weekly instead of bi-weekly won't reduce the term of your P&I home loan a great deal. The reason again is that you won't make any extra payments each year. This can be illustrated by using our previous example of a $250,000 loan at 6% interest again.

I said that if you made twelve equal sized monthly payments of $1,498.88 each year, you would pay $17,986.56 per year toward your home loan:

i.e., $1,498.88 x 12-months = $17,986.56

Again, if you choose to divide this monthly figure ($1,498.88) in half and pay bi-weekly, this is the result:

i.e., $749.44 x 26 bi-weekly payments = $19,485.44

If you compare the figures for both repayment methods, you get a difference of $1,498.88 - which equates to one extra month's repayment per year - which is the reason the term of the loan is reduced.

i.e., $19,485.44 - $17,986.56 = $1,498.88 = 1 month's extra repayment.

Now, if you divide this bi-weekly figure of $749.44 in half again to make weekly repayments, this is the result:

$374.72 x 52 weeks = $19,485.44

You can see that by paying weekly rather than bi-weekly, you won't actually make any extra repayments because there are still only 52 weeks in a year. However, you would reduce the P&I loan term from 24-years and 6-months down to 24-years and 5-months because the Daily Balance would be reduced weekly rather than bi-weekly.

Making lump sum payments

Another common method of accelerating loan reduction familiar to most people is to make lump sum payments toward their P&I Loan. For example, let's say you get a tax refund of $5,000 and you decide to put this toward our $250,000 home loan in May of the first year.

What would happen is that the Daily Balance for May would be reduced by an extra $5,000, and this would shorten the overall term of our $250,000 loan from Jan. 01, 2043 to July 01, 2041 (assuming you financed on Jan. 01, 2012). That's a time reduction of 1-year and 6-months with an interest saving of $23,223.45 based on the monthly repayment method.

Increasing your repayments

Of course increasing the amount of your monthly payments will also reduce the Daily Balance every month and cut your loan term. **Example:** $250,000 loan at 6% interest with monthly payments of $1,498.88 ...

If you were to increase your payments by $50 to $1,548.88 per month, you would shorten the overall term of our $250,000 loan from Jan. 01, 2043 to July 01, 2040. That's a time reduction of 2-years and 6-months with an interest saving of $28,660.47 based on the monthly repayment method.

The conclusion most people have come to is that there is no way to reduce their P&I home loan faster unless they make extra payments or happen to come across a windfall and make a lump sum payment toward their P&I Loan. However, that's where knowing how to use the Speed Equity® Mortgage Acceleration System to take full mathematical advantage of our Key Banking Principle can help you, and we will explore that next.

SUMMARY

The traditional, outdated methods of accelerating loan reduction familiar to most people are:

1. Making BI-WEEKLY repayments.
2. Making WEEKLY repayments.
3. Making LUMP SUM repayments.
4. INCREASING your repayments.

These traditional methods of mortgage acceleration do serve to reduce the term of a P&I loan and consequently save you interest. However, we will now explore a repayment method that hundreds of thousands of ordinary people are using all over the world to achieve spectacular results to slash years off their home loans and save tens to hundreds of $1,000's in interest.

"If you do what you've always done,
you'll get what you've always gotten."

- Linda Coleman-Willis -

The SECRET to Using the Key Banking Principle to Slash Years Off Your Home Loan & Saving Tens to Hundreds of $1,000s in Interest

*"If you focus on the problem, you can't see the solution.
See what no one else sees. See what everyone else chooses
not to see out of fear, conformity, and laziness."*

- Dr. Patch Adams -

Getting ahead financially

If you want to improve your financial position in life, there are really only two ways to do it:

1. **WORK HARDER to earn extra money, or**

2. **WORK SMARTER and make more effective and efficient use of your existing financial resources.**

I want you to think back to Chapter 3 where I outlined four of the seven traits that millionaires share in common. Do you remember one of those traits was that millionaires, **"Allocate their time, energy, AND money efficiently in ways conducive to building wealth?"** In other words, they learned to work smart instead of working hard. And that's exactly what I am about to show you how to do in applying the Speed Equity® Mortgage Acceleration System to Own Your Home Years Sooner & Retire Debt Free. You will do this by learning how to take full mathematical advantage of our Key Banking Principle. So here we go ...

If we know that ...

The Key Banking Principle

The interest on your mortgage is calculate on the DAILY OUTSTANDING BALANCE and charged at the end of the month (called monthly in arrears).

The $1 MILLION question is ...

How do you make the Key Banking Principle work for you to pay the least amount of interest?

Ans: By keeping the Daily Balance of your home loan as low as possible.

However, as you now know, this is impossible to do if you are forced to take out a P&I loan and service it by having your income going into a separate checking account and being forced to make monthly payments from it ... that in turn only reduces the Daily Interest charged on your P&I loan by pennies at a time. And remember, it's all about those humble little pennies.

Consequently, with a 30-year P&I loan you end up paying for two houses with your hard earned money but only get to keep one.

So how do you keep the daily balance low?

Ans: Use the Speed Equity® Mortgage Acceleration System.

Folks, this is as simple as I can make the explanation. Take a look at Fig. 7 (below) and I'll explain what's going on.

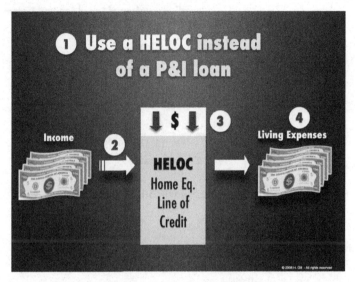

Fig. 7: The mechanics of the Speed Equity® System.

The mechanics of the Speed Equity® Mortgage Acceleration System (Fig. 7):

1. Instead of a taking out a P&I loan, you can use a different type of home loan called a Home Equity Line of Credit (HELOC).

2. That's because with a HELOC, you can directly transfer all your savings, surplus funds and income directly into it rather than having those funds sitting in a separate checking or savings account.

3. By doing the above, you will take full mathematical advantage of the Key Banking Principle because you will immediately reduce the Daily Balance of your mortgage by the amount of money you inject into it. Remember, it's all about those pennies.

4. The best part is that with a HELOC, you can draw out your money for living expenses from your mortgage as needed - on call.

As you can see, the concept is certainly not rocket science. However, the impact this has in terms of helping you Own Your Home Years Sooner and saving you tens to hundreds of $1,000's in interest is dynamite.

Case Study

The following is a real life case study from my coaching days in 1996. It shows how an ordinary couple learned to work smarter to reduce the term of their home loan and saved $93,773 in interest in the process. You'll notice that the loan amount is quite small compared to today's standards. However we are talking about 1996 when a $100,000 home loan was pretty much equivalent to a $250,000 one today.

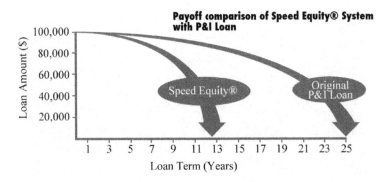

Fig. 8: Case Study - Bill & Greta

Scenario

LOAN AMOUNT:	$100,000
INTEREST RATE:	10% (that's right, interest rates were that high back then)
INCOME:	$39,000 per year
LOAN TERM:	Reduced from 25-years down to 12-years 7-months
INTEREST SAVINGS:	$93,773

Bill & Greta took out a $100,000 P&I loan with monthly payments of $908.70. However, I taught this couple how to use this System to reduce their home loan from 25-years down to 12-years 7-months and they saved $93,773 in interest.

Bill was a diesel mechanic in his forties, on an income of $32,000 per annum, and his wife Greta worked part time and earned $7,000 per year. As you can see, we're not talking about high rollers here. These are ordinary people whom you would call the 'salt of the earth'.

Their bank told them that their existing home loan of $100,000 would take them nearly 25-years to pay off. Their last mortgage statement showed that they had only reduced their home loan by $1,127 in the previous 12-months, *even though* they had paid a total of $11,572 in payments to the bank. This was a situation with which they were totally fed up with and wanted to improve upon.

To remedy this, Bill considered working away from home in a remote mining town in Western Australia so he could earn more money, and Greta thought about getting a full time job. These prospects neither of them desired because they had two young children to take care of and they wanted to bring them up jointly - not with one parent being away for most of the year. In other words, like many people, they felt they had to work harder to earn extra money, in order to make extra payments on their home loan to pay it off sooner.

However, by taking full mathematical advantage of the Key Banking Principle outlined in this book and making more effective and efficient use of their existing financial resources, they were well on their way to Owning Their Home Years Sooner and saved $93,773 in interest. Furthermore, they did this without having to change their existing lifestyle - a lifestyle with which they were very happy. Let me share with you, step-by-step what they did to become mortgage free years sooner ...

The old way of making their mortgage payments

In order to service their original Principal and Interest loan, Bill & Greta - like most people - had been taught, encouraged and brainwashed into structuring their personal finances and loan repayment in the following manner:

1. Bill & Greta's income went into a checking/savings account.

2. At the end of each month they wrote a check to their lender from their checking account to service their home loan.

3. The amount left in the checking/savings account was then used for living expenses and the rest of the money stayed in their account for 'emergency' use (see diagram below ... looks familiar, doesn't it?)

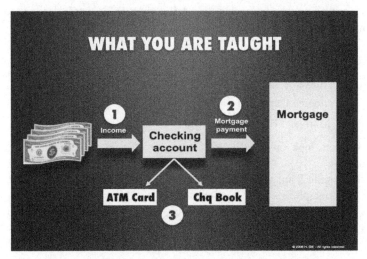

Fig. 8: The old, outdated way of servicing a mortgage.

If you are making your home loan repayments in the same way as Bill & Greta once did, then you are not making the most efficient use of your money, time and energy. That's because the money that sits in your checking/savings account for living expenses and emergency use is 'dead' money, as it earns nil to very little interest (around 1% - 2%), which in turn is taxed at your marginal tax rate. Meanwhile, the banks make their profits by taking your money and lending it back out at a much higher interest rate in the form of home and personal loans ... at a 10% interest rate in this case.

The Speed Equity® way of making mortgage payments

Bill & Greta wanted to work smarter, not harder. So, they applied the Speed Equity® System and refinanced to a type of home loan that maximized our Key Banking Principle to their advantage. Consequently, they changed their repayment structure from a traditional P&I loan to a HELOC.

As you saw in Fig. 7, this type of home loan enabled them to have all of their income paid directly into their mortgage, thus having the effect of immediately reducing the Daily Balance of their home loan by the amount of income that went into it. It also gave them the flexibility to withdraw their money 'at call' without incurring any costs whatsoever. Basically, I am talking about turning your home loan into a day-to-day transaction account with an ATM card and checkbook access.

When used in conjunction with a personalized Speed Equity® Plan (Step 2), which is a critical part of this System, this method can drastically shorten the term of your home loan. That's because every cent you deposit into your home loan now works to save you interest by reducing your Daily Balance. And remember, it's all about those humble little pennies.

Let's move on now and examine, in detail, how Bill & Greta's decision to use the Speed Equity® Mortgage Acceleration System worked for them.

STEP 1

Jan	1	Mortgage Owing	$100,000
	2	Income Deposited	-$1,200
		Mortgage Balance	= $98,800

Bill & Greta took out a HELOC on the 1st of January for $100,000 at an interest rate of 10%. Immediately, they put their bi-weekly income of $1,200 into their home loan, which reduced it down to $98,800. Remember our Key Banking Principle: interest is calculated on the Daily Balance. So from that point on, until they withdrew any money, the interest was calculated on the Daily Balance of $98,800.

STEP 2

Jan 2	Mortgage Owing	100,000
	Income Deposited	-$1,200
	Mortgage Balance	= $98,800

Jan 3	Withdraw Budgeted Weekly	
	Expenses	+$270
	Mortgage Balance	= $99,070

On the 3rd of January, they withdrew $270 for their weekly budgeted expenses in accordance with their Speed Equity® Plan, and their HELOC balance increased to $99,070 - interest was now calculated on this Daily Balance. Notice that each time they withdrew money from their home loan, it increased the amount they owed, and whenever they deposited money into their home loan, it decreased the amount they owed?

STEP 3

Jan 3	Mortgage Balance	$99,070
10	Withdraw Budgeted Weekly	
	Expenses	+$270
	Mortgage Balance	= $99,340
Jan 16	Income Deposited	-$1,200
	Mortgage Balance	= $98,140

On the 10th of January, they once again withdrew their budgeted weekly expenses of $270, which increased the home loan to $99,340. On the 16th of January, their regular bi-weekly income of $1,200 was deposited into the home loan, which reduced it to $98,140 - and the interest was calculated on this Daily Balance until the next transaction took place.

STEP 4

Jan 16	Mortgage Balance	$98,140
17	Withdraw Weekly Expenses	+$270
	Mortgage Balance	= $98,410
Jan 24	Withdraw Weekly Expenses	+$270
30	Withdraw Money for Bills	+$250
	Income Deposited	-$1,200
	Mortgage Balance	= $97,730

Jan 31	Mortgage Balance	= $97,730
	Withdraw Weekly Expenses	+$270
	Interest Deducted	+$839
	Mortgage Balance	+ $98,839

The process of income going in and expenses coming out of their new loan continued until the end of the month when the bank deducted $839 in interest from Bill and Greta's HELOC.

Recap

Let's take a moment to recap the difference between the Speed Equity® System of loan repayment compared with a traditional P&I loan.

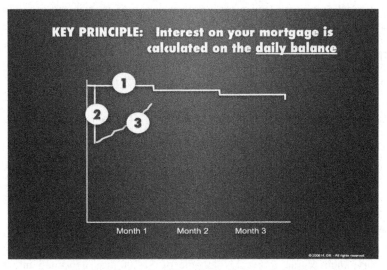

Fig. 9: Summary of Speed Equity® vs. P&I loan

1. Interest on a mortgage is calculated on the Daily Balance and charged monthly in arrears. With a P&I loan, you are only able to make periodic payments toward your mortgage. Consequently, your Daily Balance remains high and stays the same for the entire month until you make your next payment. As a result, a large chunk of your payments are consumed by the interest charged on the loan rather than reducing the loan balance. This cycle keeps you enslaved to your mortgage for the next 30-years.

2. By contrast, with the Speed Equity® System, you utilize a different type of loan, called a Home Equity Line of Credit (HELOC) that allows you to deposit your income and any surplus funds directly into your mortgage. This has the effect of immediately reducing your Daily Balance, and therefore, reducing the amount of interest you pay. Remember, it's all about those pennies!

3. The best part is that you can take your money back out for living expenses as needed. This is something you are NOT able to do with a traditional P&I loan because once you make your payment, those funds are locked into your loan.

Right now, I also need to point out some major characteristics of this type of loan.

First, you are only required to make the interest payments on a HELOC, which is calculated on the fluctuating Daily Balances throughout each month. This is unlike a P&I Loan where you are required to make set, regular repayments.

So the question that begs asking is ...

How is the HELOC balance reduced if you're only making interest payments?

By utilizing the Speed Equity® Mortgage Acceleration System, you end up saving interest in two (2) ways:

1. The money you don't use stays in your mortgage to keep your Daily Balance low for the following month. Next ...

2. The money you do need, also saves you interest by keeping the AVERAGE Daily Balance of your mortgage down for the month until you use those funds.

3. These interest savings ACT AS A PRINCIPAL REDUCTION toward your loan.

4. It is the combination of the interest savings PLUS the surplus funds left in the HELOC that accelerates the pay down of this loan to a $0 balance.

As you can see from our example, this couple decreased the principal of their P&I loan by $1,161 after only the first month - remember on the 1st of January they owed $100,000, but by the 31st of January they owed $98,839.

This $1,161 principal reduction at the end of January was achieved by having all of their income deposited into their HELOC, only withdrawing their budgeted living expenses in accordance with their Speed Equity® Plan, and leaving all of their surplus funds in the loan. These funds, instead of sitting in their checking/savings account earning them negligible interest, were now working much, much harder for them by reducing the interest payable on their home loan at the rate of 10% - *tax free!*

Again, here's what happened in January:

Total Income:	$3,600
Total Budgeted Living Expenses:	- $1,600
Interest Deducted:	- $839 (less interest than P&I loan)
Surplus Income for January:	+$1,161

Therefore, $100,000 - $1,161 = $98,839 (the HELOC balance at the end of January).

Let's have a look at what happened in the second month (February).

February

Feb	1	Mortgage Balance	$98,839
	7	Withdraw Weekly Expenses	+$270
		Mortgage Balance	= $99,109
Feb	13	Income Deposited	- $1,200
		Mortgage Balance	= $97,909
Feb	14	Withdraw Weekly Expenses	+ $270
		Mortgage Balance	= $98,179
Feb	21	Withdraw Weekly Expenses	+ $270
		Mortgage Balance	= $98,449
Feb	27	Income Deposited	- $1,200
		Mortgage Balance	= $97,249
Feb	28	Mortgage Balance	= $97,249
		Withdraw Money for Bills	+ $239
		Interest Deducted	+ $755
		Mortgage Balance	= $98,243

As you can see, by the end of the second month this couple had reduced their loan by $1,757 - that's more than they had been able to achieve in the *entire previous year!* What's more, they had not changed their lifestyle and were still living on the same amount of money to which they had become accustomed.

Although I have only shown the cash flow for the first two months for Bill & Greta, their outgoings did fluctuate due to periodic expenses, such as bills for electricity, telephone, gas, etc. This is where having the right financial tool (more on this in Step 2 "Creating Your Plan") is critical because it allows you to take into account fluctuating expense items to stay on track with your projected loan term. In the case of Bill & Greta, by switching over to the Speed Equity® System and using a HELOC, they reduced their 25-year P&I loan down to 12-years 7-months and saved $93,773 in interest - all without changing their existing financial lifestyle.

Table 8 on the next page shows a comparison of their original P&I loan repayment method with the Speed Equity® Mortgage Acceleration System.

End Year	P&I Loan Balance	Speed Equity® Loan Balance
1	$99,053	$97,150
2	$98,007	$93,682
3	$96,851	$89,516
5	$94,164	$78,738
10	$84,562	$34,473
11	$81,998	$21,791
12	$79,166	$7,484
13	**$76,037**	**$0.00**

Table 8: Comparison of P&I loan pmt. method vs. Speed Equity® System

As you can see, using the Speed Equity® System, Bill & Greta's original $100,000 mortgage was completely paid off at the end of year thirteen. Meanwhile, had they continued to repay this loan via the P&I repayment method, they would still have owed $76,037 in principle at the end of year thirteen that would have taken them another 12-years to pay off.

 **INSIDER SECRET**

What's really going on here?

Well folks, you just learned how to completely demolish the way banks make their profits.

Remember, they do this by paying out low rates of interest to you on *your* savings/ checking account. They then use fractional banking to multiply *your* money and lend those funds back out in the form of personal and home loans at a much higher interest rate. By understanding and taking full mathematical advantage of our Key Banking Principle, you will be using *your* money much more effectively and efficiently instead of allowing the banks to use it. And remember, it's all about those pennies.

For example, when Bill and Greta had their surplus funds sitting in their checking/savings account, they were earning 1.35% interest on these funds, which were then taxed at their marginal tax rate. When they started depositing these funds into their HELOC instead, they began to save 10% in interest on the equivalent amount on their home loan - and they did NOT have to pay any tax because they were saving interest instead of earning interest. I really want to emphasize this point, so I'm going to use a simple example to illustrate what I mean.

Let's say Bill and Greta had $2,000 in their checking/savings account, which they had accumulated for a vacation. This $2,000 was earning them 1.35% in interest, which they had to pay tax on at their marginal tax rate.

By transferring that $2,000 into their HELOC until they needed it, they would reduce their loan by this amount of money. This means they would now save interest at the rate of 10% on $2,000 of their HELOC, which is really the same as earning 10% on the $2,000 that was previously sitting in their checking/savings account. The best part is, they don't have to pay any tax on this increased 'return' because they are saving interest as opposed to earning interest. Are you beginning to see the power of those pennies?

In effect, you are using your existing cash flow to take away the bank's ability to make a profit and using those very same funds to Own Your Home Years Sooner instead.

Finally, by using the Speed Equity® Mortgage Acceleration System, you will be doing exactly what millionaires do. And that is; **"Allocating YOUR time, YOUR energy, AND YOUR money efficiently in ways conducive to building wealth?"**

In the remaining chapters, I will take you through a number of different case studies that build your knowledge on how this type of loan has been successfully used by thousands upon thousands of people to become mortgage and debt free years sooner. And remember ...

 ## BEWARE: DO NOT rush off & refinance your P&I loan to a HELOC

At this stage some of you are probably thinking; "Wait a minute Harj. I just refinanced my mortgage to a fantastic 30-year fixed interest rate recently. Now you're asking me spend $1,000's more to refi again into a HELOC?"

ABSOLUTELY NOT!

Remember, we're still in Step 1: "Learn How" whereby I'm still walking you through this concept step-by-step and I DO NOT want you to refinance your perfectly good 30-year fixed interest rate P&I loan and spend $1,000's to do so.

In fact, I'm going to show you how to implement this System WITHOUT having to refinance your existing P&I loan and WITHOUT having to spend any money. More on that as you read on.

"Seeing is a rather curious thing for
the alternatives have always existed.
So if we were not able to see them,
then this is because they did not fit our
logic and our theory of what ought to exist."

\- Herbst -

Step 1: Chapter 10
Slashing Years Off A Home Loan - Case Study

"The buck stops with the guy who signs the checks."

- Rupert Murdoch -

This chapter outlines in more detail how another couple - David and Sheryl - used the Speed Equity® System to reduce the term of their home loan from 20-years 4-months down to 9-years 11-months and saved $83,216 in interest.

Case Study - David & Sheryl

LOAN AMOUNT:	$101,313
INCOME:	$36,000 per year
LOAN TERM:	Reduced from 20-years 4-months to 9-years and 11-months
INTEREST SAVINGS:	$83,216

Rather than having their income go into a checking account, David and Sheryl also took out a HELOC into which they directly transferred all of their income. This had the immediate effect of reducing the Daily Balance of their home loan, and of course, interest was then calculated on the reduced loan amount.

Table 9 on the next page illustrates, in detail, how this couples' home loan reduced from $101,313 to $96,941 over the first 12-month period. It shows their first year's monthly loan balances according to their personalised Speed Equity® Plan. As you can see, based on their financial lifestyle at the time, their results showed:

1. How much interest they had to pay on their home loan at the end of each month, and their Monthly Closing Balances for their HELOC.

2. As I mentioned in the previous chapter, HELOCs are *interest-only* loans. So, David & Sheryl were only required to make interest-only payments on their mortgage, which varied according to their Daily Balance. Therefore, the figures in their Speed Equity® Plan were critically important because they acted as guideposts as to how much they should pay off their home loan at any given time. It was like having a *financial GPS* to payoff their mortgage years sooner. I will explain why this is so crucial in Step 2 ("Creating Your Plan"), but right now I want you to focus on getting the workings of our Key Banking Principle squarely ingrained in your mind.

3. Again, this couple only withdrew their budgeted living expenses as shown in the results of their Speed Equity® Plan. And it was the combination of the interest savings PLUS their surplus funds left in their HELOC that reduced it over the 12-month period (see Table 9).

Cash Flow Forecast: David & Sheryl

	Jan	Feb	Mar	Apr	May	Jun	Jul	Aug	Sep	Oct	Nov	Dec
Opening Balance	101,313	100,980	100,387	99,866	99,143	98,659	97,926	97,833	97,268	97,493	97,281	96,756
Income:	2483	2483	2483	2483	2483	2483	2483	2483	2483	2483	2483	2483
Expenses												
Property Taxes	0	0	0	0	0	0	0	0	474	0	0	0
Water Rates	0	0	0	0	0	0	445	0	0	0	0	0
Electricity	70	0	50	0	70	0	70	0	70	0	70	0
Gas	0	72	0	0	72	0	0	72	0	0	72	0
Telephone	0	75	0	0	75	0	0	75	0	0	75	0
Home Maintenance	20	20	20	20	20	20	20	20	20	20	20	20
House Insurance	0	0	0	0	0	0	0	0	0	0	0	500
Food & Groceries	542	542	542	542	542	542	542	542	542	542	542	542
Clothing & Footwear	20	20	20	20	20	20	20	20	20	20	20	20
Newspapers/Magazines	13	13	13	13	13	13	13	13	13	13	13	13
Alcohol Tobacco	10	10	10	10	10	10	10	10	10	10	10	10
Health Insurance	50	50	50	50	50	50	50	50	50	50	50	50
Gifts	20	20	20	20	0	0	0	0	0	0	0	0
X-mas	0	0	0	0	0	0	0	0	0	0	0	400
Entertainment	20	20	20	20	20	20	20	20	20	20	20	20
Holidays	0	0	0	0	0	0	0	0	0	500	0	0
School Expenses	87	87	87	87	87	87	87	87	87	87	87	87
Accounting Fees	0	0	0	0	0	0	500	0	0	0	0	0
Miscellaneous	108	108	108	108	108	108	108	108	108	108	108	108
Vehicle 1 Insurance	0	0	0	0	0	0	0	0	418	0	0	0
Vehicle 1 Registration	258	0	0	0	0	0	0	0	0	0	0	0
Vehicle 1 Fuel/Oil	90	90	90	90	90	90	90	90	90	90	90	90
Vehicle 1 Service	0	0	0	100	0	0	0	0	0	0	0	0
INTEREST CHARGED	842	783	832	800	822	790	815	811	786	811	781	808
Closing Balance	100,980	100,387	99,866	99,143	98,659	97,926	97,833	97,268	97,493	97,281	96,756	96,941

Table 9: Case study - David & Sheryl

To get an exact idea of how much time and interest they could save, David & Sheryl created a personalized Speed Equity® Plan to compare the results of using the System with their original P&I loan repayment method. Their calculations showed the following:

End Year	P&I Loan Balance	Speed Equity® Loan Balance
1	$99,671	$96,941
2	$97,866	$91,722
3	$95,870	$85,327
4	$93,667	$77,769
5	$91,236	$68,902
6	$88,553	$58,565
7	$85,593	$46,577
8	$82,325	$32,738
9	$78,719	$16,826
10	**$74,739**	**$0**
11	$70,347	$0
12	$65,499	$0
13	$60,150	$0
14	$54,246	$0
15	$47,730	$0
16	$40,539	$0
17	$32,603	$0
18	$23,845	$0
19	$14,180	$0
20	$3,512	$0
21	$0	$0

Table 10: Comparison of P&I loan repayment method vs.
Speed Equity® System for David & Sheryl

David & Sheryl's Speed Equity® Plan showed that if they maintained their current lifestyle and used the Speed Equity® System, they would completely pay off their $101,313 home loan by the end of the 10th year (9-years 11-months to be exact) with an interest saving of $83,216.

This loan would have taken them 20-years and 4-months to pay out using their original P&I loan repayment method, and by the end of the 10th year, they would still have owed $74,739 of the principal - *plus* interest!

What about future expenses?

One of the great characteristics of a HELOC is that it allows you to withdraw funds back up to the original limit of the loan at any time, without you having to spend thousands of dollars reapplying for finance. David and Sheryl loved this feature because they were planning to spend $10,000 on renovating their home in February of the 5th year of their loan.

However, they also realized that now, every time they withdrew money they hadn't accounted for, it would affect the term of their loan and the amount of interest they would eventually pay. Therefore, they wanted to make an informed decision as to whether it was worth spending this money and increasing the term of their loan. To help them arrive at this decision, they used the software to create a "WHAT-IF" scenario based on withdrawing $10,000 in February of the fifth year of their HELOC.

The analysis showed that with the $10,000 expense in year five of the loan, it would increase their loan term from 9-years 11-months to 10-years and 11-months. This meant they could now make an informed decision as to whether this expense was worth extending their home loan for another 12-months.

In other words, they were in total control of their finances – which is also a trait that all millionaires share in common ... and I'll show you how to do that in Step 2 ("Creating Your Plan").

"Do just once what others say you can't do, and you will never pay attention to their limitations again."

- James R. Cook -

Step 1: Chapter 11
Making Wise Choices

"Life is a series of choices and,
It's up to us to make wise choices."

- Morrel Perry -

Based on my investigations over the years, I have found that every country in the world has unique characteristics and quirks in terms of their mortgage and banking industries and therefore, the types of loan products they offer. Regardless of the lending infrastructure of a particular country, I am able to work out how to modify the execution of this System to suit - within reason of course. For example, when I was contacted by homeowners in Malaysia, I had to teach them how to adapt the Speed Equity® System to work within the parameters of their banking system ... same with the South Africans, Singaporeans and the English.

In this chapter, I am going to detail how to apply my Speed Equity® System specifically for the United States. First, let me take a moment to outline some very unique features of the U.S. mortgage and banking industries. Not many people know this but the U.S. is the only country in the world where you can:

1. Claim your mortgage interest as a tax-deduction (although not for long).

2. Fix the interest rate on your P&I loan for 30-years.

Each of the above variables represented challenges I had to overcome in order to teach people to let go of holding on to a 30-year mortgage. I addressed the first challenge in Chapter 5 ("The Great American Mortgage Tax Deductibility Scam). In terms of the second variable, a lot of people have an aversion to an Adjustable Rate Mortgage (ARM) that - "may" - be unfounded depending on their particular circumstances and needs. My personal adage regarding mortgages is that ...

> *"There is no such thing as a bad loan product. Only bad choices made by people that were not given sufficient knowledge and education to manage it properly."*

In order to help you make an informed decision as to what's right for you, allow me take a moment to give you a ...

Brief history

Prior to 1980, American banks and savings and loan associations (S&Ls) lent their own money to borrowers, usually at fixed rates between 6-7%. Then in the late 1970s, rate restrictions on the banking industry were lifted, and soon after that, inflation rose to 14%. This led to short-term interest rates going even higher, with the prime rate reaching as high as a staggering 23%.

You didn't have to be a rocket scientist to see that anyone lending out money at a fixed rate of 6% and having to pay 14% to a depositor who supported the loan was not going to stay in business for very long. In fact, a lot of lenders who had been around for some time did go under, merged, or were taken over and liquidated for this very reason.

As a result, lenders and regulators alike acknowledged that an alternative had to be found for lending out volatile short-term funds, and the Variable Rate Mortgages (VRM) or Adjustable Rate Mortgages (ARMs) were born. These types of loans essentially lock in a lender's profit margin at a specific rate, let's say 2%. That is, if the lender pays their depositors 4% then they will lend you that money at 6%. If they pay depositors 6.5% then they will lend you that money at 8.5%, and so on.

Taking this approach, regulators ensured that 'Portfolio Lenders' (institutions lending against their depositor's funds and keeping the loans 'in house') would not endanger themselves by going under amidst a volatile interest rate environment.

Rise of the secondary market

The problem that arose as a result of the VRMs and ARMs was that borrowers still wanted long term fixed rate loans, but the lenders, who were mostly portfolio lenders, did not want to offer them anymore. Consequently, this demand for fixed rate loans gave rise to what is now called the 'Secondary Mortgage Market'.

What happened is that quasi-governmental companies such as the Federal National Mortgage Association (FNMA), commonly known as 'Fannie Mae' and the Federal Home Loan Mortgage Corporation (FHLMC), called 'Freddie Mac', stepped in to fill the void left by the portfolio lenders. These companies buy fixed rate mortgages from banks, S&Ls, and mortgage bankers. They then package them into 'pools' that might total $10 or $20 million, and then sell interest in the pools to institutional investors such as pension plans and mutual funds.

There is a lot more to this story, but for our purposes, it's sufficient to say that this is the way the secondary market provides liquidity to the primary lending market. It is the means by which your local bank, S&L, or mortgage banker can offer long term fixed rate loans that it originates.

Consequently, you will find that soon after you take out your home loan, you will find yourself mailing your mortgage payment to a company other than the one that originated your loan. That's because in 95% of cases, U.S. mortgage companies no longer lend you their own money. They simply package loans that they can then sell to some other company immediately or at some time in the near future.

What does this have to do with you?

Ans: everything.

One of the things you must realize is that the interest rate of a HELOC (or any Revolving Line of Credit type of loan) is ALWAYS tied to the variable interest rate because in most cases, only portfolio lenders originate these types of loans.

Again, because lenders secure the loans against their depositor's funds, they have to ensure that they retain a profit margin in order to protect themselves from any potential rises in interest rates. Therefore, you can expect the interest rate of your HELOC to fluctuate during the time you have it. The only exception is that some lenders may offer a fixed introductory interest rate for a short period of time in order to win your business, and then, the loan will revert to whatever the variable rate happens to be after the fixed rate term has expired.

After reading thus far, you might think that in order to Own Your Home Years Sooner, you have to refinance your entire P&I loan to a Home Equity Line of Credit (HELOC) and then apply the Speed Equity® concept as you have learned. That is not the case.

You see, I deliberately structured my book this way so as not to go into the intricacies of the execution of the concept too soon. That's because I wanted you to stay focused on getting the workings of the Key Banking Principle down pat first. Now that I believe you have a good handle on this concept, I can reveal to you that in actual fact, you have three options you can exercise to apply this System - all of which have their own unique pros and cons. These options are:

1. Convert your entire P&I loan to a HELOC
2. Take out a smaller HELOC as a 2nd mortgage (recommended)
3. Use a Personal Line of Credit (PLOC)

Notice, that no matter which option you choose you have to utilize a Revolving Line of Credit type loan? That's because at present, the North American banking system only offers this type of loan product to make the Speed Equity® Mortgage Acceleration System executable. Let's now examine each of the three options above.

OPTION 1 - Convert your entire P&I loan to a HELOC

This option is just like the scenarios I described in Chapters 9 and 10. With this approach, you would convert your entire P&I loan to a HELOC and then apply this System to reduce it quicker.

Once your HELOC is set up this way, all of your income is paid into your HELOC as well as any savings are transferred into it. This has the immediate effect of reducing your loan's Daily Balance by the amount of income that goes into it, thus decreasing the amount of interest you are charged. You then treat your HELOC as a day-to-day transaction account whereby you withdraw your budgeted expenses in accordance with your Speed Equity® Plan via an ATM Card and checkbook as required, and leave the rest of your funds in the HELOC (see Fig. 10 below).

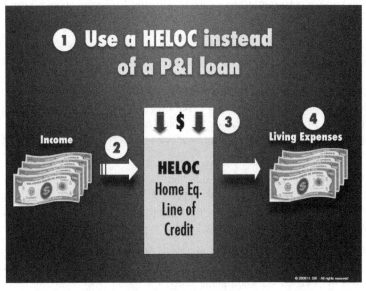

Fig. 10: The mechanics of the Speed Equity® System.

If you choose to apply Option 1, here are the advantages AND disadvantages associated with this approach:

Advantages:

• In all honesty, in the United States, I cannot think of any worthwhile advantages to this approach that you cannot achieve with Option-2. However, there are numerous …

Disadvantages:

▪ You will be exposing your entire loan amount to the variable interest rate. For example, for every $100,000 of mortgage debt, a 1% increase in the interest rate will result in an extra $1,000 in interest cost PER YEAR! That means if you replace your perfectly good fixed interest rate mortgage with a first lien HELOC and interest rates go up by a full 1% and … your daily balance throughout the year is at least $300,000, then you can expect to pay $3,000 in extra interest for the first year and EVERY

SUBSEQUENT YEAR your daily balance is at least $300,000.

- If you don't have a plan and the right tools to give you monthly benchmarks to manage this type of loan properly, you will never pay it off because your only obligation is to pay the interest each month.

- You can keep drawing the funds right up to the original approved loan amount at any time. Therefore it's particularly dangerous for those of you that are not willing to take pro-active control of your mortgage and personal finances.

 ## WARNING to U.S. homeowners

Personally, I think being able to fix the interest rate on a P&I loan for 30-years is a FANTASTIC option. I still remember when my parents were forced to pay 18% interest on their mortgage back in the 80's. That put tremendous stress on their marriage and our family as a whole. Given the choice, I would take out a 30-year P&I loan with a fixed interest rate of 5.25%, in a heartbeat because I'm extremely conservative and like to control as many variables as I can that will impact my future. Knowing that the interest rate on my mortgage is stable for as long as possible would give me tremendous peace of mind.

Therefore, I must STRONGLY CAUTION you to BEWARE of anyone trying to convince you that you have to refinance or Replace Your Mortgage to apply this concept. These folk are using, I would go as far to say abusing, this concept to refinance people out of perfectly good fixed interest rate P&I loans into their "special" loans based on the "Australian System" - that's how they market it. You DO NOT have to do this!

The reason these companies want you to do this is because they get paid hefty commissions, on top of their up-front fees, but ... ONLY IF they refinance you into their loan product.

Again, DO NOT do this!

My job here is to educate you and help you get out of debt - NOT - to put you into more debt and/or put your financial future in jeopardy.

You might be thinking, *"Ok Harj, now I'm totally confused. You said I have to take out a HELOC to make this System work - which has a variable interest rate. However, you're saying personally, you would take out a 30-year fixed rate P&I loan that is NOT implementable with this System? What gives?"*

Actually, there's nothing to be confused about and certainly no contradiction in what I am saying. Now that you understand the concept, it's time to get down to the execution. So let's examine ...

OPTION 2 - Take out a smaller HELOC as a 2nd mortgage (recommended)

I highly recommend this option because it has major advantages over Option 1.

That is, rather than refinancing your entire P&I loan to a HELOC, you would apply for a smaller HELOC as a second mortgage and then implement the Speed Equity® Mortgage Acceleration System to reduce it quicker. This is also the option I would personally exercise in the U.S. By the way, this DOES NOT apply to anyone outside of the U.S. and I explain this in detail, in the relevant country editions of this book. In other words, one size DOES NOT fit all. So please, don't be fooled into thinking you're getting the best methodology to execute this concept just because it works somewhere else.

Now, let's take a look at how this can be set up to work using a ...

Case Study - Jim and Marylyn

PROFILE

HOME LOAN (P&I):	$150,000
INTEREST RATE:	Fixed @ 6.0%
MONTHLY PAYMENT:	$899.33
LOAN TERM:	30 years
APPRAISED VALUE OF HOME:	$250,000

Jim and Marylyn had a $150,000 P&I loan, which they had secured a fixed interest rate for 30-years at 6.0%, and they were making monthly payments of $899.33 toward it.

They worked out that if they refinanced their entire P&I loan amount as a HELOC and applied the Speed Equity® System, they could Own Their Home in less than half the time and save $94,347 in interest.

However, they did not want to give up the security of the fixed interest rate on their P&I loan, but still wanted to apply this System to reduce their home loan quicker.

The great news is that if you are in a similar predicament, there is a perfectly workable solution that gives you the best of both worlds. That is, you can take out a smaller HELOC as a second mortgage, to which you apply the Speed Equity® System, while leaving the larger portion of your home loan at the fixed rate as a P&I loan. The best part is that you can still achieve virtually identical results as Option 1 by doing this. The other advantage is that there are absolutely NO REFINANCING COSTS involved and you can set up this whole process for almost $0.

The following is what Jim and Marylyn did. I know it may look confusing at first, but it's not. Just follow the numbered explanations in the diagrams, and reread this section several times if you have to because this is most likely what you will choose to do also. As I said, this is also the option that I would personally exercise in the U.S.

Step 1: They empowered themselves with knowledge and made a commitment to make the Speed Equity® System work in their lives.

Step 2: They created a personalized Speed Equity® Plan, which showed them exactly how much time and interest they would save by subscribing to the Speed Equity® System - compared to their original P&I loan repayment method.

Step 3: They applied for a smaller HELOC as a second mortgage that in turn allowed them to apply the Speed Equity® System WITHOUT having to refinance and at virtually $0 cost.

Jim and Marylyn worked out that they had enough equity in their home to qualify for a HELOC with a $50,000 credit limit as a second mortgage (I'll show you how to work that out a bit later). However, they didn't want or need to access this entire amount of equity, so they only applied for a HELOC with a $40,000 credit limit - also available to them at 6.0% (see Fig. 11 below).

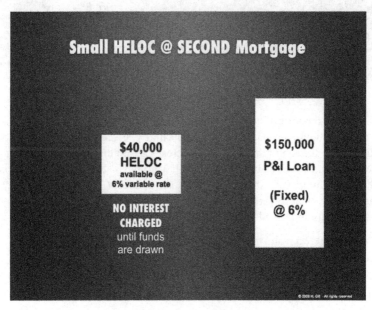

Fig. 11: OPTION 2 = small HELOC as 2ⁿᵈ mortgage

Next, they wrote a check from their HELOC for $5,000 and made a lump sum injection into their P&I loan that brought it down to $145,000. Incidentally, only the portion of the HELOC that is drawn down is charged interest - in this case, interest is payable on only $5,000 (see Fig. 12 on the next page).

By the way, the reason they did not lump sum the entire $40,000 into their P&I loan was because they wanted to have a 'safety-buffer-fund' in case of emergencies. And second, they only wanted to expose a very small portion of their mortgage debt load to the variable interest rate - which is exactly what I would do.

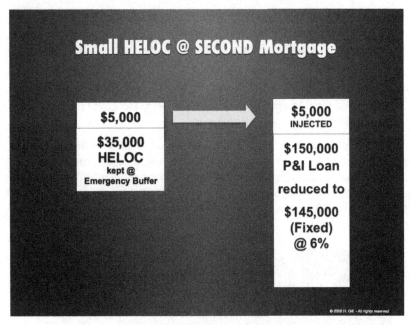

Fig. 12: Injecting small portion of HELOC into P&I loan

At this stage, the immediate ramifications of this action are obvious. That is, if you made a lump sum payment of $5,000 into your P&I loan, of course you would reduce the loan term and save interest - assuming you kept making the same repayments. For example, in Jim and Marylyn's case, when they injected $5,000 as a lump sum into their P&I loan and kept making their $899.33 monthly repayment toward it, it had the effect of reducing their P&I loan by 2-years 5-months and saved them $21,067 in interest. I hear you ask ...

> *"But wait, all you've done is transfer the debt from the P&I loan over to the HELOC, and you're expecting me to believe that this is going to save me all that time and interest?"*

"Ahh, outstanding question", I say, and here's more of the story.

Yes, they did transfer $5,000 of debt from their original P&I loan over to a HELOC.

However, they could now take full advantage of the Key Banking Principle by depositing all of their income into the HELOC portion of their mortgage, thereby reducing the amount of interest they were charged. This was something they were not able to do had they stayed with their original P&I loan.

The outcome was that they are now depositing all of their income into their HELOC and only withdrawing money as they need it, according to their Speed Equity® Plan. They are also maintaining their $899.33 monthly payment toward their P&I loan from the HELOC (see Fig. 13 on the next page).

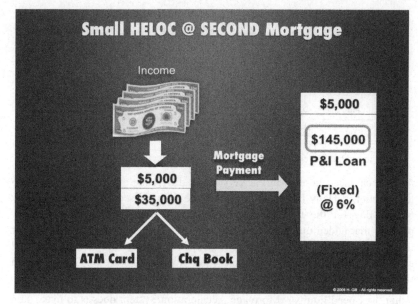

Fig. 13: Paying down HELOC using Speed Equity® method

In effect, what they are doing is focusing all their attention on paying off the $5,000 HELOC as fast as they can by using the Speed Equity® System, without significantly changing their lifestyle. When they reduce the $5,000 HELOC down to a $0 balance, their personalized plan tells them when that will be, they will make another lump sum payment from it into their fixed rate P&I loan and start the whole process again.

This will of course reduce their P&I loan by another $5,000, and by maintaining the $899.33 monthly payment toward it, it will again significantly reduce the P&I loan term accordingly. Remember Jim and Marylyn are now gaining a two-fold advantage with their hard earned money:

1. They are accelerating the reduction of their P&I loan every time they make a lump sum injection into it from their HELOC.

2. They are saving interest on the HELOC portion of their mortgage debt because they are taking full mathematical advantage of our Key Banking Principle to reduce the amount of interest they are charged.

They will keep repeating this process until both loans are completely paid off.

Is it really worth the effort?

The next question, sometimes a criticism, people usually have is that the amount of interest savings are so small on the HELOC that it hardly seems like a worthwhile exercise. Well, let's just take another look at Table 3 from Chapter 7 ("Your Prison Made From Pennies") shall we? Remember the Daily Interest charged for our $250,000 P&I loan?

Month	Daily Balance	Daily Interest Charged	Difference in Daily Int. Charged
Jan	$250,000.00	$41.09	
Feb	$249,775.09	$41.06	- 3¢ per day
Mar	$249,425.86	$41.00	- 6¢ per day
Apr	$249,198.03	$40.96	- 4¢ per day

Table 3: Daily Interest Charged on $250,000 mortgage over first four months

As you can see, there is only a very small difference of 3¢ per day between the amount of Daily Interest charged for the first and second month, and only 6¢ per day for the next month. Friends, remember it was these itty-bitty pennies that added up to $289,596 in interest over the course of 30-years for this $250,000 P&I loan. I also told you that bankers and lenders are well aware of this fact, and they also know that most people pay very little interest (again, no pun intended) to these humble little pennies.

What the Speed Equity® Mortgage Acceleration System does is to make sure that these itty-bitty pennies stay in your pocket, so that you are not at the mercy of compound interest.

In this case example, by making the decision to use the Speed Equity® System, Jim and Marylyn are well on their way to Owning Their Home Years Sooner - and saving $94,347 in interest.

What's the cost of two separate loans?

Aaaahh, another excellent question and I'm so glad you asked.

Ans: very little "IF" you setup your Speed Equity® Plan properly. Let's recap using Fig. 14 below.

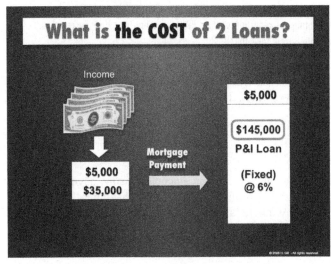

Fig. 14: Paying down HELOC using Speed Equity® System

As you can see, we had a HELOC with a $40,000 credit limit from which we injected $5,000 into our $150,000 fixed-rate P&I loan. This had the effect of immediately reducing the Daily Balance of that P&I loan down to $145,000.

We then continued to make monthly payments to the P&I loan and simultaneously, utilized the Speed Equity® Mortgage Acceleration System by injecting all our income into the HELOC portion of the mortgage debt to keep the Daily Balance as low as possible.

At this stage we need to make a couple of assumptions:

1. We have $4,000 of after tax income that can be injected into the HELOC every month.

2. The HELOC interest rate is 6.0%

Based on the above, take a look at what's going on in Fig. 15 (below).

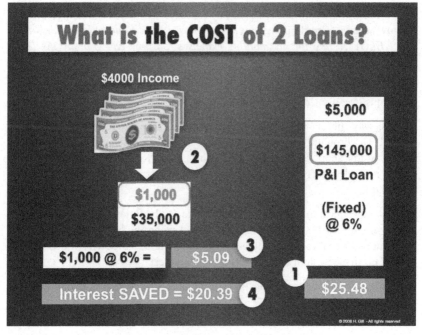

Fig. 15: The cost of having two separate loans

There are a couple of moving parts here, but again, it's very easy to understand if you follow the numbered explanations.

1. If we hadn't injected $5,000 from the HELOC into the P&I loan, we would have had to pay 6% interest on the entire $5,000 left in the P&I loan. For the month of January, that would have ended up costing us a total of $25.48 in interest. But remember, we "transferred" this $5,000 debt into the HELOC portion of our mortgage.

2. Now, we owe $5,000 on the HELOC. However, we also have $4,000 of income that is injected into it from day one. Therefore, we are only paying interest on a HELOC debt of $1,000 (i.e. $5,000 owed on HELOC - $4,000 income injected into HELOC = $1,000 Daily Balance). Therefore ...

3. That amounts to a total of $5.09 in interest payable for the month of January.

4. The interest saved is $20.39 for the month of January - which acts as a principal reduction for the HELOC.

So, let me ask you a question. Would you be able to find $5.09 to save $20.39 in interest? And may I remind you that it's all about those itty-bitty pennies?

Therefore, the answer to your question, "what's the cost of two separate loans" is not much - "IF" - you setup your Speed Equity® Plan properly.

I know what you're thinking now, *"But Harj, I have to drawdown funds from the HELOC to pay for my monthly expenses. So how can you say the Daily Balance is going to remain at $1,000 for the entire month?"*

Boy, you guys are a tough audience but ... I'm glad you're asking such great questions because I'd be doing the same.

By the way, please indulge me. Even though I'm a proud American Citizen now, I was brought up on a diet of very dry Australian humor that still runs strong in my veins. Besides, I warned you in the "Read Me First" section that this is not a dry stuffy textbook on finance but more of a conversation between you and I.

Back to the question regarding keeping the Daily Balance at $1,000 for the entire month ... I'll show you how to do that using the bank's money and - at absolutely $0 cost to you - in the next Chapter called "SECRETS to Using the Speed Equity® System to Save Even More Interest".

I know you have one more question for me in this section. And that is ...

What if the HELOC interest rate increases?

Let's examine that shall we?

Take a look at Fig. 16 (next page) and once again, just follow the numbered explanations.

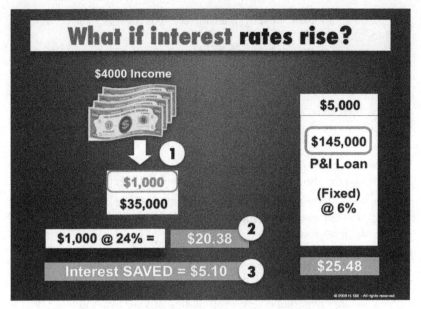

Fig. 16: What-if the HELOC interest rate increases?

1. We are only paying interest on a HELOC debt of $1,000 (i.e. $5,000 owed on HELOC - $4,000 income injected into HELOC = $1,000 Daily Balance).

2. If the HELOC interest rate increases to 24% (the maximum amount I have seen in a HELOC contract), the interest payable for the month of January would be $20.38

3. We would still save $5.10 interest for the month of January - which acts as a principal reduction for the HELOC. Need I say again ... it's all about those itty-bitty pennies.

Overview

Let me finish this section by taking you through a brief summary of what Jim and Marylyn did.

- They thoroughly educated themselves and decided that they wanted to apply the Speed Equity® System to Own Their Home Years Sooner.

- They created a personalized Speed Equity® Plan that showed them exactly how much time and interest they would save by subscribing to the Speed Equity® Way compared to their P&I loan repayment method - without significantly changing their lifestyle.

- They applied for and were approved for a $40,000 HELOC credit limit which enabled them to apply the Speed Equity® System in their lives.

- Once they got their HELOC, they injected $5,000 from it into their

$150,000 P&I loan, thereby immediately reducing its balance down to $145,000.

- By continuing to make $899.33 monthly repayment toward their P&I loan from the HELOC (after injecting $5,000 into it) it initially reduced the P&I loan term by 2-years 5-months and saved them $21,067 in interest.

- They then deposited ALL their income into their HELOC and only withdrew money as they needed, in accordance with their Speed Equity® Plan.

- Once they paid off their HELOC down to a $0 balance, they made another lump sum injection of $5,000 from it into their P&I loan.

- They will keep repeating this cycle until both loans are completely paid off, which in their case will result in a total time saving of over 15-years and $94,347 in interest.

Advantages

✓ You can achieve the SAME RESULTS as Option-1.

✓ You are only exposing a very small portion of your total mortgage debt to the variable interest rate. Therefore, any increases in the prime rate will have a MINIMAL IMPACT on your total interest cost … this is in contrast to Option-1 whereby even a small increase in the interest rate will result in a significant increase in your mortgage interest cost.

✓ You will still be required to make regular payments toward your P&I loan. Therefore, the worst-case scenario is that you will still pay off your mortgage in accordance with your original P&I loan amortization schedule.

✓ If you find this concept is not working for you, you can always go back to your original P&I repayment method without having to refinance and incur any costs to do so.

✓ You can use the HELOC exactly as described to pay off any debt, especially high interest bearing ones, before applying it to your home loan.

✓ From a psychological standpoint, the smaller HELOC amount will seem like a manageable sized loan that you will see being eliminated very quickly, right before your eyes, which in turn will give you more motivation to achieve the forecasted results of your Speed Equity® Plan.

✓ Easy to setup because you are not refinancing your entire P&I loan amount.

✓ 2nd lien HELOC setup costs are very low and in most cases $0.

Disadvantages:

▪ You must have a cash flow management tool to calculate exactly HOW MUCH of a HELOC Credit Limit to apply for, the exact LUMP SUM AMOUNT to inject into your P&I loan and … precisely WHEN to make those injections to save the maximum amount of time and interest.

- You can keep drawing funds right up to the original HELOC Credit Limit at any time.

- If you don't have a personalized plan and the right tools to give you monthly benchmarks to manage your HELOC, you will never pay it off because your only obligation is to pay the interest each month.

Moving right along, let's now examine the pros and cons of ...

BEWARE of The Fearmongering About 2nd Lien HELOCs

The companies that want you to purchase their first lien HELOC solution will tell you that a 2nd lien HELOC can be shut down ... as per what happened from 2009-2015 in the U.S. when we were in the middle of the housing crisis.

This actually happened to some personal friends of mine, in the Las Vegas area, even though they had plenty of equity.

Here's what really happened ...

Most lenders had a knee jerk reaction to the downturn in housing values by shutting down second lien HELOCs. The reason they did so was obvious ... i.e. they did not want you to draw down equity from your home that you did not have.

So, instead of examining every case individually to see if you were over leveraged or not, they simply pulled up all the zip codes with the highest reduction in home values and shut down HELOCs in those zip codes en masse ... regardless of how much equity you had.

By the way, that was completely illegal as lenders are required to provide a valid reason for shutting down your access to credit. However, we were dealing with a very serious issue with global consequences and lenders simply reacted with short sighted, short-term solutions.

The million dollar question is ... "Could this happen again?"

The short answer to that is a categorical ... NO!

Why?

Because that was a complete anomaly in the U.S. housing market, which should never happen again. Hence the creation of the Consumer Financial Protection Bureau ... aka CFPB.

One of the CFPB's jobs is to regulate how mortgages are originated so home loans are only approved to those borrowers that are able to afford them thus ... stabilizing the housing market.

In other words, "IF" we ever see a situation like that happen again, then we're all sunk and ... you'd better have plenty of canned food and bottled water stored in your basement because we're going to bring down the entire global financial system with us.

The real question you should be asking is; "Why does the guy that invented this concept promote Option-2 in the U.S. and charges significantly less than his competitors?

Answer: I want you to implement this System correctly, safely, and especially ... WITHOUT having to pay an extra penny of interest that you don't have to because there is absolutely no financial gain for me to recommend this approach.

Moving right along, let's examine the pros and cons of ...

OPTION 3 - Using a Personal Line of Credit (PLOC)

If you find that you can't qualify for a HELOC because your Loan to Valuation ratio exceeds what a lender is agreeable to - which is the case for at least 19% of mortgaged households in the U.S. at the moment - then you may be tempted to apply for a Personal Line of Credit (PLOC) to apply with the Speed Equity® System.

From a technical standpoint, this is absolutely doable because you will be using a revolving line of credit, and you would follow exactly the same steps as I outlined in Option 2. However, from a practical standpoint I only recommend it in extreme situations ... more about that in a moment.

Advantages

✓ This is UNSECURED DEBT. That means you do not have to offer your home as collateral/security to the bank. Therefore, there is no need for appraisals, inspections and all the hassle that goes with trying to get a 2nd lien HELOC.

✓ PLOC setup costs are $0.

Disadvantages

▪ The only drawback to using a PLOC is the interest rate will be significantly higher than a HELOC because this type of revolving credit is not secured against your property. How much higher will depend on the lender you decide to apply for your PLOC with and other factors such as, your credit history and score. However, if you "manage/control" your daily balance correctly, the higher interest rate won't matter.

▪ Other than that, all of the other advantages and disadvantages are the same as Option 2.

Now let me tell you about the client that proved me wrong about using a PLOC with this System ...

CASE STUDY

In 2017 I got a call from a gentleman in Augusta, GA.

He had scoured YouTube for ways to pay off his mortgage sooner and really wanted to get started with my System ASAP. He told me that he didn't have enough equity to qualify for a HELOC to use with it just yet so ... I told him to wait until he did.

A few weeks later I was informed that he went ahead and purchased the Speed Equity® Software anyway.

I immediately called him and asked why he had gone against my recommendation to wait?

This is what transpired in that conversation:

Me: *"[Client] you're paying 10.75% interest on the PLOC when the current HELOC interest rate is 3.5%. Why didn't you wait to get a HELOC like I told you to?"*

Client: *"Harj, you teach in this book that it's not the interest rate that matters but controlling the daily balance."*

Me: *"That is correct."*

Client: *"Well, even though I'll be paying almost three times the interest rate on my PLOC compared to a HELOC, I'll still pay off my mortgage 21-years sooner and save over $85,000 in interest. So, I'm not waiting!"*

He went on to explain that he had spent hours using my software to calculate exactly how to control the daily balance of his PLOC to pay the least amount of interest on it.

At this stage I realized there wasn't much point trying to convince him otherwise so ... I made him promise to stay in touch each month to keep me informed of his progress.

Well, six months go by and he had built up enough equity to qualify for a HELOC ... so I called him to say he should now apply for one.

Here's the kicker ... he said; *"No thanks. I'll stick with using my PLOC."*

Me: *"But why?"*

Client: *"Well, my PLOC has worked out just fine for me and I'm not interested in handing over my home as collateral to the bank by using a HELOC. Besides, I use your software each month to stay on course to pay the least amount of interest on it so I'm good."*

The only retort I had was to say; *"In over 22-years of teaching this System, I have never seen anyone so diligent and committed to making it work."*

I also promised him that I would modify all future editions of my book and reference his personal experience.

In other words, he followed my 3-Steps to the letter and proved that even without the optimal loan product (HELOC) one can still make this System work.

I guess slashing 21-years off his loan term and saving over $85,000 in interest was motivation enough for him.

Now, there is one more option I'd like to discuss here and I'll call it . . .

OPTION 4 - The completely INSANE Option ... use a Credit Card

Again from a technical standpoint this is doable because a credit card is nothing more than a line of credit. However, you would have to be completely out of your gourd to even consider it because it is fraught with so much danger.

I first heard about this practice in 2009.

As I explained, that's when many U.S. lenders were having a knee jerk reaction to the mortgage crisis and freezing people's HELOCs en masse, purely based on their zip codes, regardless of whether their credit and service history were in good standing. Suffice to say, that many of the companies that jumped onto the mortgage acceleration bandwagon panicked and started instructing their clients to apply for a PLOC because they couldn't qualify for a HELOC. And then, when the PLOCs started to dry up, they started telling people to use Credit Cards instead!

Folks, this is what I mean about absolutely abusing, if not downright prostituting, this concept to make a quick buck at the expense of innocent homeowners. I hope the reasons for NOT exercising this completely INSANE OPTION are clearly obvious, but if not, let me outline the main points for you:

1. Pulling money out from your Credit Card rather than using it to make a purchase is considered a "cash-advance" and you are immediately charged the MAXIMUM interest rate. In most cases up to 25%.

2. You only have to miss your credit card payment one time and you will not only end up with a huge ding on your credit report, but also hit with an exorbitant late charge - not to mention having your credit card frozen or having its credit limit reduced.

Therefore, I say to you DO NOT, and I repeat, DO NOT even entertain the thought of exercising this option. Furthermore, stay right away from anyone that tells you to do so because they will do nothing more than put you at extreme financial risk.

While we're here, I might as well tell you about ...

OPTION 5 - The B.S. Option ... You can use your checking or savings account instead of a HELOC

I really had to do a double take when I heard this one. Again, because of the number of American households that are upside down on their mortgage and cannot qualify for a HELOC, this approach is being touted as a completely viable alternative to apply the mortgage acceleration concept you just learned.

The proponents of this approach reckon they have "figured out a way", using magical algorithms, for you to use your checking or savings account to achieve spectacular results in not only helping you pay off your mortgage, but also to eliminate all your debts. Here's the lowdown of their methodology:

1. Use their magical algorithm based software to help you accumulate surplus funds in your saving or checking account.

2. Wait for their magical algorithm based software to tell you when and how much of those accumulated surplus funds to inject into your P&I loan and watch it vanish before your eyes.

Hmmmm, didn't we already discuss this in Chapter 8 ("Traditional Outdated Methods of Loan Reduction)?

In case you haven't figured it out already, this is NOT taking advantage of our Key Banking Principle and it is certainly NOT about interest cancellation.

In fact, it is nowhere close.

The travesty is that these charlatans want to charge you hundreds of dollars every month for nothing more than a simple budgeting software.

If this is what you want to do, then you can do it yourself with MS Money or any number of budgeting software programs available on the internet for FREE.

Do you see why I call it the B.S. Option?

"People and organizations frequently hold on to faulty assumptions about their world for as long as a decade, despite overwhelming evidence that it has changed and they probably should too."

- Andrew Pettigrew -

I'm sure you will agree that conceptually, the idea of mortgage acceleration upon which the Speed Equity® System is founded, in its pure form is very, very simple. However, when it comes to executing the theory, there are all sorts of variables that need to be taken into account and more than enough scoundrels you have to avoid lest you fall under their spell and find yourself being parted with your hard earned cash.

In this chapter, I hope that you are clear as to the options available to bring this System to life so you too can Own Your Home Years Sooner and save tens to hundreds of $1,000's in interest. Those options are:

OPTION 1:	Convert your entire P&I loan to a HELOC
OPTION 2:	Take out a smaller HELOC as a 2nd mortgage (recommended)
OPTION 3:	Use a Personal Line of Credit (PLOC)

And make sure you stay completely away from ...

OPTION 4:	The INSANE Option ... Use a Credit Card
OPTION 5:	The B.S. Option ... You Can Use Your Checking or Savings Account Instead of a HELOC

In closing this chapter, I also hope that you do not mind my "Australian" sense of humor and candor in telling it like it is. If I offended you in any way I do sincerely apologize. At least now you know if you would ever want to invite me over to your house to throw another shrimp on the barbie.

Now, let's take a look at how we can really turbo-charge your interest savings in the next chapter.

"You don't have to be great to get started,
but you have to get started to be great."

- Les Brown -

Step 1: Chapter 12
SECRETS to Using the Speed Equity® Mortgage Acceleration System to Save Even More Interest

"Many people take no care of their money till they
come nearly to the end of it. And others
do just the same with their time."

- Goethe -

In this chapter, I will show you how to save even more interest by taking further advantage of our Key Banking Principle including some unique methods my readers and past clients have come up with.

Using the bank's money to reduce your HELOC interest - *at absolutely $0 cost to you!*

Most people will tell you that the advent of credit cards was perhaps one of the worst things that ever happened to human beings. We have all heard horror stories of people owing large sums of money on credit cards and being charged exorbitant interest rates. However, it is my firm belief that credit cards per se are not at fault, but rather the way people use/abuse them. Because when used wisely, they can actually reward AND save you interest.

As you know, a lot of things can now be purchased on a 20 to 30-day interest free credit card. This means that you are not charged interest for the purchases until the interest free or 'grace' period is over.

Many people using the Speed Equity® System are also using a credit card for their day-to-day budgeted living expenses, as per their Speed Equity® Plans, and paying for their purchases within the interest free period (see Fig. 17 below).

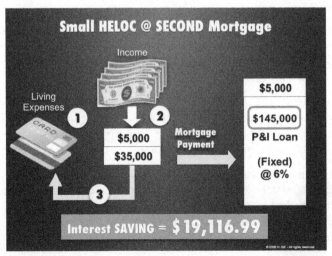

Fig. 17: Using the Bank's money to reduce your HELOC interest at $0 cost to you

Here's a step-by-step explanation of what's happening in Fig. 17

1. Use the bank's money for your monthly living expenses via credit card, while ...

2. Your money is left in your HELOC - which reduces your Daily Balance - and therefore reduces the amount of interest you have to pay.

3. When you get your credit card statement at the end of the month, pay it off IN-FULL by writing a check from your HELOC or using online banking.

If you just did this one-time only ... that is, you injected $4,000 of income into your HELOC, used a credit card for your monthly expenses - let's say that added up to $4,000 - then completely paid off your credit card at the end of the month from the HELOC, and did nothing more with the Speed Equity® System ever, you would save a whopping $19,116.99 in interest with a $250,000 loan at 6%. How? It's all about those pennies. Tell me, where else can you get a guaranteed ROI like that at absolutely $0 cost to you?

Furthermore, using a credit card will also help you to refine the forecast of your Speed Equity® Plan because you will get an itemized statement of your living expenses each month that you can then use to update your Speed Equity® Plan with.

A word of caution

If you have had trouble-managing credit cards in the past, then DO NOT use the process I just described. The personalised Speed Equity® Plan you will create in Step 2 deliberately DOES NOT include the use of credit cards. Using them to defer living expenses is just an added bonus.

However, if you have the self-discipline to handle credit cards and pay them off monthly, then you will be pleased to learn of other ingenious uses with which some of my readers have found.

Using 'smart money'

Once Steve & Elena setup their HELOC and discovered how easily and quickly they could reduce the term of their home loan, they started to look for more ways to save interest. Besides using credit cards for their budgeted living expenses, here's what they came up with.

Steve was a golfing fanatic and played a round every Saturday with his buddies. Collectively, they spend nearly $200 a week on golf. Steve collected cash from his golfing partners for their green fees and paid for the group with his credit card - which also earned him reward points.

At the first opportunity, he went to the bank and deposited this money into his HELOC, which immediately reduced his principal and therefore reduced the amount of interest he had to pay. In effect, Steve used the bank's money to save even more interest on his HELOC and paid it back within the interest free period with absolutely no cost to him.

Steve & Elena also did the same thing whenever they went out to dinner with their friends. They decided to carry very little cash with them and preferred to have their money working for them by leaving it in their HELOC because it's all about those pennies.

Grocery shopping

Sherry has an elderly mother that she does the grocery shopping for every week. Her mother pays her cash for the groceries, and Sherry then charges them to her credit card. She deposits her mother's money into her HELOC straight away and pays for the groceries when she receives her credit card statement at the end of the month. She jokingly said she was thinking of doing the shopping for the entire retirement village this way.

If you don't have a relative you can do this for, then why not go shopping with your neighbor or friend and pay for their groceries on your credit card, and get them to give you the cash? If you're really brave, you can offer to do this for the person in front of you in line at the store.

Difference between charge, debit, and credit cards

A 'Charge Card' carries no pre-set spending limit, and the statement balance must be paid in full at the end of the billing cycle (usually every month). The most recognized charge cards on the market today are American Express® and Diners Club®. A 'Debit Card' is like an ATM card that you have attached to your savings or checking account. With this type of card, you must have funds in the card account before you can make a withdrawal. In contrast, a 'Credit Card' carries a pre-set credit limit, and only a minimum (principal and interest) payment is required to be paid each month, and interest is applied to balances not cleared or paid in full.

Who are VISA® and MasterCard®?

These are the two major independent institutions that make the whole credit/debit card transaction system work.

Note that just because you have a VISA® or MasterCard® logo on your card does not mean that it's a 'Credit Card'. For example, you can have a VISA® Debit Card issued by your bank that allows you to take out cash from an ATM displaying the VISA® symbol and also to have it accepted by merchants like a regular credit card. This option gives you the best of both worlds - i.e., ability to take out cash and use it to buy goods. The only thing that you have to ensure is that the card account has sufficient funds in it at all times.

Who are MAESTRO® and CIRRUS®?

MAESTRO® is an international EFTPOS (Electronic Funds Transfer Point Of Sale) system. It let's you use your Maestro® Card to buy goods and services at any outlet displaying the Maestro® logo. You can also withdraw cash from an ATM displaying the Maestro® logo because it accesses the funds directly from your checking or savings account. CIRRUS® is an international ATM network. With your Cirrus® Card, you can withdraw cash and obtain account balances (in the local currency), at any ATM in the world displaying the Cirrus® logo.

Whenever using credit cards ...

As I have pointed out, if you are thinking about using credit cards to defer payment for your living expenses then here are the things you need to be aware of:

- A lot of people make the mistake of thinking that just because they have a credit card, they also automatically have an interest free period attached to it. This is NOT the case, so make sure that the credit card you have comes with an interest free or 'grace' period (usually around 20-30 days). Otherwise, you will be charged interest from the moment you make a purchase.

- Get a credit card with an interest free period that does not charge you a high account-keeping fee ($0 - $30 per year is average).

- Never, ever use your credit card to withdraw cash. This is considered to be a "cash-advance" (a loan), and your bank will charge you interest at the maximum rate, up to 29%, from the moment you make the transaction.

- Always pay the credit card bill as soon as you get your statement. DO NOT, and I repeat, DO NOT, try to fiddle with the remaining interest free days to delay payment right up until the last moment. I know people that have forgotten to pay, or they couldn't make it to the bank on the last day, and of course they are then hit with the interest, an exorbitant late charge and a possible ding on their credit report. However, I have observed that most people only do this once.

Diamonds in your backyard

Another way people have accelerated their Speed Equity® Plan is by selling unwanted household items and then injecting this money into their HELOCs.

It's surprising how much you can make with those unnecessary items lying around your home. And before you think they have no value and take them to the dump, just remember the adage, "One man's trash is another man's treasure." You can offload these things through a simple garage sale, consignment store, or even through eBay, which is always a lot of fun. Simon & Fiona (one of my coaching clients from 1996) did this, made $954 and cut another 4-months off of their projected Speed Equity® Plan - which also saved them another 4-months worth of interest. So, how many diamonds can you find in your backyard?

How to get a loan for at least 3% below the variable home loan interest rate

You may have noticed that the interest you earn on your savings account is always a lot less than the interest you are charged on your home loan - because that's how banks make their profits.

However, another one of my clients from my coaching days, Steve, used this knowledge to his advantage to save a lot of money on his HELOC.

This is what he did.

His parents had nearly $19,000 in a cash management account earning 3.5% interest, and he had a large HELOC costing him 9.9%. That worked out to be a difference of 6.4% i.e., 9.9% HELOC - 3.5% Cash Management Account = 6.4% in favor of the bank.

Steve's personalised Speed Equity® Plan showed him that if he injected $19,000 into his HELOC and paid his parents the same interest they were earning with their cash management account, he would be the one coming out 6.4% in front.

That worked out to be a saving of over $100 in interest each and every month, which really meant $100 extra coming off of the principal of his HELOC each month.

Steve explained this to his parents and asked them if they planned to use their $19,000 in the near future. They said it was "for a rainy day" and liked the idea of having the money available to them 'at call'.

Steve then explained to them that he had a Speed Equity® Plan that he was using in conjunction with a HELOC - which in turn doubled as his personal day-to-day transaction account. He told them that if they put their money into his "bank", he would pay them the same interest as their current cash management account, and they would still have the money available to them 'at call' - albeit through his HELOC.

Steve's parents were only too glad to help out since there was absolutely no difference to them in terms of the returns on their savings.

In effect, this method cost Steve 3.5% interest on $19,000 of his HELOC rather than 9.9% - not a bad interest rate for a loan, wouldn't you say? And even if he had paid his parents 4.5% interest, he would still have been 5.4% better off.

Having said all that, you can see that this case example is from the years when interest rates were a lot higher than at the time of this publication. Therefore, although the savings are not going to be as great during the periods when interest rates are low, it is a good ace to keep up your sleeve if interest rates take a turn for the worse - which they eventually will as part of the historical economic cycle.

BEWARE: when borrowing money from friends & family

Be fully aware that if you call any form of document a 'credit contract', or if you do something that makes the transaction have the appearance of you being in the business of lending money, that you could be violating certain state and/or federal regulations. So, please be careful in the way that you go about writing the repayment schedule to avoid this situation.

Furthermore, this particular method relies heavily on trust, and you don't want to lose friends and family members because of conflict over money.

Therefore, if you are thinking of doing anything remotely like this, you may want to do the following to avoid potential conflicts:

✓ Never try to force anyone to lend you the money. If you have explained how the Speed Equity® System works, they have read this book, and they still feel uncomfortable with the idea, let them be. It's their money after all.

✓ No matter who it is, or how close you are to your 'lender', ALWAYS, and I mean ALWAYS, have the contract in writing. Make sure you outline the amount being borrowed and the terms and conditions of the 'loan'. Include how much interest you will pay the lender, when the interest will be paid, by what method it will be paid, and how the lender can have access to the money if and when they need it. Furthermore, it is a good idea to have a lawyer review this document to make sure it is sound.

✓ Finally, don't spend the interest savings. Stay within your projected monthly budget according to your Speed Equity® Plan, and leave the surplus in your HELOC. If your lender wants the money 'at call', you won't know when that call may come. But until it does, use the injected funds wisely because the interest you save will now be reducing the principal of your home loan.

"Learning is not attained by chance, it must be sought for with ardor and attended to with diligence."

- Abigail Adams -

Step 2: Chapter 13
The Crucial Importance of Creating Your
Personalized Speed Equity® Mortgage Acceleration Plan

"Start where you are. Use what you have. Do what you can."

- Arthur Ashe -

How much time and interest will you save when using the Speed Equity® System?

One of the first questions I am always asked, especially in media interviews is; *"Harj, how much time and interest can people save using your System?"* And my response is always; *"I don't know!"*

The reason, I explain, is because we are no longer talking about a traditional P&I loan. That type of mortgage always has a preset amortization schedule that is predetermined for you by your lender along with a fixed monthly repayment amount. In which case, you don't have to concern yourself with anything other than writing a check for your regular monthly payments or authorizing an automatic deduction from your bank account. Besides that, there is absolutely nothing you have to do except make sure you have a job for the next 30-years to keep servicing your ball and chain P&I loan.

In contrast, when using the Speed Equity® System, what we are talking about is *you* taking total control of *your* mortgage to derive full mathematical advantage of the Key Banking Principle so *you* can save the maximum amount of time and interest. As a result, *you* get to determine how much interest *you* want to save and how long *you* want to take to Own Your Home Years Sooner. In the interviews, I elaborate by saying, *"what I can tell you is that based on the data I gathered from home loan borrowers using my System, the:*

Average Interest Saving:	= $109,293
Average Time Saving:	= 16 years

I conclude by stating that the amount of interest that you will save when using the Speed Equity® Mortgage Acceleration System depends on four (4) factors that are unique to each individual. And they are:

1. The size of *YOUR* home loan
2. The amount of *YOUR* Current Debts
3. The amount of *YOUR* Income and
4. The amount of *YOUR* Regular Expenses

Putting together all the pieces
I need you to pay particular attention to this section because I am going to bring together the explanation of several interconnected moving parts.

Remember the key to saving the maximum amount of time and interest on your mortgage when using the Speed Equity® System is knowing that the interest on it is calculated on the daily balance and charged monthly in arrears. Therefore, what you want to aim for is having as much money as you can sitting in your HELOC for as long as you can, thereby reducing the amount of daily interest you are charged and have to pay. In essence, we are talking about turning your home loan into a day-to-day transaction account with income going in and expenses coming out of it.

You also know that with a HELOC, your only obligation is to service the interest on this type of loan each month. Therefore, the question I posed was:

How is your HELOC balance paid off if you're ONLY making interest-only payments?

Ans: by utilizing the Speed Equity® System with a HELOC, you end up saving interest in two (2) ways that accelerates the payoff of your mortgage:

1. The money you don't use stays in your mortgage to keep your Daily Balance low for the following month. Next ...

2. The money you do need, also saves you interest by keeping the AVERAGE Daily Balance of your mortgage down for the month until you use those funds.

3. These interest savings act as a PRINCIPAL REDUCTION toward your HELOC.

4. It is the COMBINATION of the interest savings PLUS the surplus funds left in your HELOC that accelerates the pay down of this type of loan to a $0 balance.

Why you MUST have a personalized Speed Equity® Mortgage Acceleration Plan

Your lender's only obligation is to tell you how much HELOC interest you have to pay each month and ... if you only pay the interest each month, you will NEVER actually pay this type of loan off – *and that's the danger!*

In my most recent Australian edition, I presented evidence that exposes how major lenders in that country are deliberately engaging in nefarious activities to enslave people to their debts for as long as possible. That's their job. Having you mismanage your HELOC would be playing directly into their agenda. Consequently, unless you have a robust management system to set AND help you achieve monthly and yearly goals with your HELOC, you will never actually know when you will, or should, pay it off. Compounding this is the fact, that a HELOC acts as a day-to-day transaction account that enables you to withdraw your funds right up to the original HELOC credit limit at any time.

Therefore, even though a HELOC is the best type of loan product to apply with the Speed Equity® System, it does require a little planning and diligence on your part. However, the rewards are well worth it. In fact, as you have seen, when the Speed Equity® System is executed properly, in conjunction with a HELOC, it can literally slash years off your home loan and save you tens to hundreds of $1,000's in interest by helping you take full mathematical advantage of our Key Banking Principle.

Consequently, *"the"* most important aspect to successfully using a HELOC with the Speed Equity® System to Own Your Home Years Sooner is to manage it properly. **That is, you have to have the right tool that helps you effectively keep track of money** going in and coming out of your HELOC as well as giving you monthly and yearly benchmarks. That's because from now on, every dollar you deposit and every dollar you withdraw from your HELOC will have a direct impact on how long it takes you to Own Your Home Years Sooner & Retire Debt Free.

Since 1995, every single homeowner I have personally seen succeed with this System did so because they created their personalized Speed Equity® Plan BEFORE they applied for their HELOC (Step 3). Their customized plan took into account *their* income, *their* expenses, *their* current debts as well as *their* planned future expenses. It then showed them exactly how much of their HELOC they should pay off at the end of each month and each year, as well as the total amount of time it would take for them to be completely mortgage free.

I can also tell you that the reason every single person I have seen fail with this System was because they tried to skip this step. They thought that somehow their interest-only HELOC would magically pay itself off. That's tantamount to the interaction Alice had with the Cheshire Cat in Lewis Carroll's fable "Alice in Wonderland" and I quote:

> *"Would you tell me please, which way I ought to go from here?", asked Alice.*
>
> *"That depends a great deal on where you want to get to", said the Cat.*
>
> *"I don't much care where', replied Alice.*
>
> *"Then it doesn't matter which way you go," said the Cat.*
>
> *" ... so long as I get somewhere", added Alice.*
>
> *"Oh you're sure to do that", said the Cat, "if you only walk long enough."*

Please note I cannot emphasize strongly enough the importance of what I am about to say:

> **If you choose not to follow through with my recommendation of creating your personalized Speed Equity® Plan, then PLEASE DO NOT GO ANY FURTHER BECAUSE YOU WILL FAIL.**

And unlike Alice, you're not going to end up wandering around a fairytale. Your potential destination could be foreclosure and destruction of your credit history - which is the last thing I want for you. So if you're not willing to follow my directive to create and manage your personalized Speed Equity®

Plan BEFORE & AFTER you get your HELOC, then just know that there is a much better way for you to Own Your Home Years Sooner & Retire Debt Free but … it's not for you.

Now that we've got the fire and brimstone speech out of the way, I'd like to take a moment to remind you of what I sketched out in terms of job security in Chapter 1 ("Why You Should Own Your Home Years Sooner As An American"). As a result of those scenarios, I also stated that each and every one of us has to take individual responsibility in order to secure our own financial future. That does not, and will not happen automatically - just as your interest-only HELOC is not going to pay itself off on its own.

Up to this point we have been engaged in Step 1 ("Learn How"), where we focused purely on the theoretical aspect of using the Speed Equity® Mortgage Acceleration System to help you take full mathematical advantage of our Key Banking Principle.

It's now time to move on to ...

Step 2: The practical application of the Speed Equity® Mortgage Acceleration System

The great news is that what I am about to teach you in this step of the Speed Equity® System ("Create Your Plan") is going to help you practically develop one of *the* most important traits that millionaires have that enabled them to create and manage their wealth. And that is, besides allocating their time, energy and money efficiently in ways conducive to building wealth ...

> Millionaires BUDGET - AND - they also PLAN their investments.

Again, unlike the funneling process of the "wealth creation" seminar industry that simply puts you on an endless cycle of workshops that cost $1,000's, yet only give you a bunch of B.S. philosophy, this step of the Speed Equity® System gives you the opportunity to put into practice what real millionaires do in terms of budgeting and planning to payoff your most expensive asset - *your home.*

"Always bear in mind that your own resolution to succeed is more important than any other."

- Abraham Lincoln -

Step 2: Chapter 14
Getting Down To Business

"When you set goals, something inside of you starts saying,
"Let's go, let's go," and the ceilings start to move up."

- Zig Ziglar -

Planning is the key

In order for us to achieve any goal in life, we must first plan for it. Planning is simply a choice we make to create a desirable future for ourselves, and the communities in which we live. We also have a choice not to do that because as William James once said:

> *"When you have to make a choice and don't make it,*
> *then that in itself is a choice."*

At certain breakpoints in our lives, just like the character, Alice, in Lewis Carrol's story, we too ask, "which way ought I to go from here?" The wise answer to that of course is, *"it depends on where we want to get to."*

Once we have decided on a destination or a goal, and we want to maximize our chances of getting there, we must prepare for the journey through the act of planning.

Simply put, planning is all about designing and bringing about a desired future that otherwise would not exist without our intervention.

It is about deciding **WHAT to do** and **HOW to do it BEFORE** action is required.

The value of goal setting and planning

Most of us have come to loathe the term planning and 'goal setting' because it reminds us too much of all the New Year's Eve resolutions that went unfulfilled. That is truly unfortunate because such continual disappointment has led many people to shy away from creating their lives according to their dreams. I must point out that this is not entirely our fault because we have never been given the proper framework or tools with which to clearly plan for, and systematically achieve a goal. I don't know about you, but I certainly was not taught this skill in school.

Well, all that is about to change because I am going to share with you *the* most potent SECRET I have discovered to plan for and systematically achieve ANY goal in life - from losing weight to climbing Mt. Everest.

IF YOU FOLLOW THIS FORMULA EXACTLY, it is an absolutely FOOLPROOF recipe for success. In fact, if you have young children, I would highly recommend that you pass this knowledge on to them because it will help them throughout their adult lives. What's more, you can use the Speed Equity® Software as a practical tool of how it is done because it was specifically created using this success planning blueprint.

So what is this SECRET, FOOLPROOF formula for success?

The method I am about to share with you is called the 'SMART' way to set and achieve goals. The acronym S.M.A.R.T. stands for:

Specific Measurable Achievable Results with a Timeframe = S.M.A.R.T.

How does this S.M.A.R.T. method work, and why is it so effective?

To answer the above question, let me clarify what I mean by goals and plans and then explain the S.M.A.R.T. components in more detail.

GOALS: The aspirations we want to achieve, or a destination we want to reach.

A PLAN: The map or set of guidelines that gets us there. Now let me elaborate on the ingredients that a 'good' plan must have in order to successfully achieve a goal.

Specific: The first ingredient in your plan that is critical in order for you to create and successfully achieve your goal is that your goal has to be specific. If you don't know EXACTLY what you want, then how can you even begin to take the steps to acquire it?

Measurable: The second necessary ingredient your plan has to have is a tangible unit of measure such as time, money, weight, etc. This is extremely important because the unit of measure you use is directly tied to how you get feedback on your progress in attaining your goal.

Achievable: Next, in order to succeed with your goal, you must have a goal that is achievable. Otherwise you will never take your plan seriously enough to carry it through. For example, there's no point in saying you want to be mortgage free in the next six months when you know for a fact that is not going to be possible.

Results with a **Timeframe**: These are two final and key components a plan must have. That's because without knowing the results you are supposed to achieve within certain timeframes, how are you going to know whether you are making any progress toward attaining your goal - and more importantly - be able to implement the necessary measures to get back on track if you are not?

The Speed Equity® Software helps you Own Your Home Years Sooner the S.M.A.R.T. way

Before I published the first Australian edition of this book in 1997, I realized that I also had to find a way for homeowners to see for themselves that the results I was talking about were absolutely achievable for them. Otherwise, they would have simply read my book and filed it away in their mind as a "nice idea".

Instead, I wanted them to take action.

And to do that, I had to provide them with a practical instrument to be able to see their own results.

The second reason, as you now know, was to give them a tool to actually achieve their individualized goals of accelerated home ownership. Without it, people would have refinanced to HELOCs en-masse, which they did, and then defaulted on them because their only requirement would have been to service the interest each month. To me, leaving people to fend for themselves like that would have been unconscionable. Thus was born …

The Speed Equity® Mortgage Acceleration Software Program

As I said, this tool is precisely based on the S.M.A.R.T. formula to help you successfully set and achieve your goal of Owning Your Home Years Sooner.

Let me take a moment to outline each of those S.M.A.R.T. ingredients in relation to this online software.

SPECIFIC: The first most valuable attribute of this software is that it CALCULATES EXACTLY, down to the penny, HOW MUCH you should inject from your HELOC into the P&I loan and precisely WHEN to make those injections to save the maximum amount of time and interest.

Fig. 18 (below) is a screenshot of the software's "Loan Term Comparisons" screen showing results of a client that saved 19-years and 10-months and $156,635.57 in interest using this software. You'll agree that it doesn't get any more SPECIFIC than that.

Fig. 18: Speed Equity® Software forecasts SPECIFIC Time & Interest savings

MEASURABLE: In terms of measurable attributes, the Speed Equity® Software gives you two interrelated units of measure. One is dollars, and the other is time. These units of measure will leave absolutely no doubt in your mind as to the progress you can and are making toward Owning Your Home Years Sooner & Retiring Debt Free.

ACHIEVABLE: As I said, one of the first questions I'm always asked in media interviews is, *"Harj, how much time and interest can people save with your System?"* I always tell them, *"I don't know because we're no longer talking about a set amortization schedule determined by your lender and therefore, the results vary from person to person."* However, this software let's you know precisely what is achievable for you with *your* income, *your* expenses, *your* current debts, *your* planned future expenses, and the size of *your* home loan. It also allows you to work out different what-if scenarios to see which ones enable you to realistically Own Your Home Years Sooner. In other words, it puts *you* in total control of *your* finances so *you* get to decide how soon *you* want to become mortgage free rather than your lender.

RESULTS with a **TIMEFRAME:** Once you enter your data, the first thing the Speed Equity® Software will do is forecast for you an end goal, a destination.

In Fig. 18 (previous page), the end goal of that homeowner was to pay off a 26-year and 6-month, $200,001 P&I loan in 6-years and 8-months and save $156,635.57 in interest. The next thing for him to do was to get to that end goal and the software guided him every step of the way. It did this via the "Cash Flow Summary" screen (see Fig. 19 below). This screen gave him his month-by-month HELOC Closing Balances and steered him to achieve those waypoints just like a GPS System ... as it will do for you.

Fig. 19 (opposite page): Speed Equity® Software Cash Flow Summary screen showing RESULTS with a TIMEFRAME as month-by-month HELOC Closing Balances

Because "LIFE happens"

Last, you know from personal experience that no matter how much planning and forecasting you do, "life-happens" whereby unforeseen circumstances are guaranteed to arise. In which case, don't worry because just like a GPS system, the Speed Equity® Software has an in-built re-rerouting mechanism that helps you get back on track if anything goes awry.

For example, let's say you have to replace your air-conditioning unit and it costs you $3,000 - an expense that you had not budgeted for in your original data input into the software, but you still have to pay for this expense from your HELOC.

What happens as a result is that your HELOC Closing Balance for that particular month would be $3,000 higher than your original forecasted closing balance.

Basically, all you would have to do in this scenario is UPDATE the ACTUAL Closing Balance of your HELOC (as shown in your loan statement for the month) in the software. It then recalibrates itself based on the ACTUAL HELOC Balance for the month and creates an UPDATED set of monthly closing balances for the ensuing months.

This is a fully dynamic function that allows you to see the impact of any unanticipated expenditure (or income) will have on your original end goal.

You can then use the "what-if" scenarios feature to work out what you need to do in order to bring yourself back on course to being mortgage free within the original forecasted time.

As I said, it's just like a GPS System that will guide you to Own Your Home Years Sooner & Retire Debt Free.

Budgeting & planning with a huge reward at the end

Some people (especially bank staff and the ill informed) will tell you that you need an iron will and superhuman discipline to manage a HELOC properly.

Well, let me dispel this inane misconception that is backed up by countless people that have already used this System and software to become mortgage free years sooner.

> The #1 reason most people don't budget, or manage a HELOC, is because they don't have the right tool to see the direct impact their cash flow can have on their loan term

I bet that like most people, whenever you spend your hard earned cash right now, you have no way of assessing how each expense affects your financial position in the future, especially in relation to paying off your home loan sooner.

I believe this simple fact alone accounts for why most people have never been able to budget, or if they have a budget, have not been able to stick to it.

In contrast, when using a second lien HELOC in conjunction with the online Speed Equity® Software, you will see a direct correlation between the income you earn and the money you spend on the overall term of your home loan (see Fig. 20 below). The best part is that it allows you to dictate how soon *you* want to Own Your Home by allowing *you* to manipulate any number of variables. For example, 'what-if' you wanted to know the effect of:

1. Depositing/withdrawing lump sum amounts in a specific month and year (e.g., depositing tax refunds, paying for renovations, holidays, etc.)?
2. Increasing/decreasing your income by $x a week/month/quarter, etc.?
3. Increasing/decreasing the interest rate?
4. Increasing/decreasing any expenses by $y a week/fortnight/month, etc.?

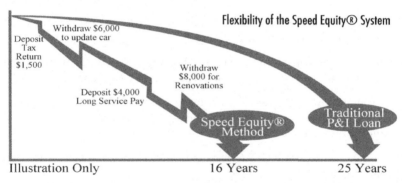

Fig. 20: Speed Equity® Software helps you create "what-if" scenarios and gives you IMMEDIATE feedback

Using the Speed Equity® Software, you will be able to accurately calculate the effect that each of these 'what-if' scenarios will have on the overall term of your home loan.

So from now on, every time you want to spend your hard earned money, you are able to make informed decisions based on facts.

You can then decide whether it would be better to spend your money now or wait until a more suitable time. I have found from personal experience that the SECRET as to why every one of my readers and personal clients who Owned Their Home Years Sooner (many exceeding their expectation) was because they used this life changing software.

Why?

Because it gives you instant feedback about the effect that your spending habits will have on the overall term of your home loan.

It actually makes the concept of "budgeting" down right fun because ... you are able to see how a simple change in your current spending could result in an extra $4,134.03 in interest savings. That is why I feel so strongly about communicating to you the importance of creating and managing your personalized Speed Equity® Plan properly. But ...

Don't take my word for it!

This recommendation is supported by an extensive study conducted by Professor Elaine Kempson from the University of Bristol in England. She is an internationally known and respected authority on consumer financial issues with over 30 years' experience of conducting research and contributing to policy development on various aspects of personal financial services, including banking, saving and investment, insurance, credit and mortgages and pensions.

Professor Kempson conducted a global research study on the financial literacy and capability of thousands of adults. In her conclusion, she said;

> "... having real-time access to your financial position and clear visibility of your spending and saving patterns can help build a sense that you are the Masters of your own destiny."

And that is why, ladies and gentlemen, Step-2 ... AND the Speed Equity® Software is so critically important in implementing this System correctly.

Step one gives you the financial literacy about this concept and Step- 2 gives you the practical management tool so you are capable of bringing it to life.

 BEWARE: of imitation software programs that give false results

Please, please be aware that there are at least fourteen companies in the U.S. that have copied my System by creating imitation "mortgage acceleration" systems but none of them have a HELOC management software that is as sophisticated and accurate as Speed Equity®.

Case Study #2: I was working with a mortgage broker in Seattle, WASHINGTON that wanted to offer my book and software to all his clients as a closing gift. Eleven months earlier, he had paid $12,000 to purchase a license from one of these fly-by-night mortgage acceleration software companies that authorized him to charge whatever he wanted to his clients ... as long as he paid them an additional $250 per account thereafter.

He decided to give a valued client a free subscription to this imitation software program. However, these clients were never able to achieve their forecasted monthly HELOC closing balances as shown in this company's software. So the mortgage broker asked me to see what *they* were doing wrong.

To cut a long story short, instead of focusing on what "his clients were doing wrong", I decided to examine the algorithms upon which the software was built. I uncovered that the programmers had built-in certain assumptions that made the results look much more "rosy" than they really were. Hence, the inaccurate and unachievable monthly HELOC closing balances for his clients. Sadly, this is not the first time I've come across this practice.

Case Study #2: In early 2018, a client called my office wanting to purchase my software. During our Discovery Call, he told me that he had actually paid $3,500 to one of my imitators in 2006.

So I asked him; *"Why in the world do you want to pay again for my System?"*

He said; *"Harj, I know this concept works because I used it pay off my first home loan. But I didn't know about you at the time so I signed up with them and ... all I got was a bunch of videos to watch and nothing to manage my HELOC with."*

He continued; *"I realized that I was doing it completely blind because I never knew when to make injections from my HELOC into the P&I loan and for what amount let alone the monthly balances I should be aiming for."*

He concluded; *"This time around, I want to do it right!"*

Unfortunately, most people are not able to tell the difference between the good, the bad, and the downright ugly mortgage acceleration software programs on the market today. When they see huge discrepancies between their actual and forecasted HELOC closing balances, they assume they must be doing something wrong rather than blaming the software because they bought it in good faith. After having parted with $1,000's with nothing to show for it, they then give up on the mortgage acceleration concept altogether … and to me that is the real tragedy of lost hope.

A letter from someone who really knows

Let me conclude this chapter by sharing with you one of the most powerful testimonials I have ever received about the effectiveness of this Software. It was actually from an investigator from the Dept. of Consumer Affairs and here's what she said about it ...

> *"I am saving $108,344.14 and paying off my home 18 years earlier than the original 30-year loan.*
>
> *"I was so close to buying into one of the $3,500 copycat systems out there ... I had put down the $500 deposit and was being asked for my credit card number a few days later to get started, when I asked, "Is there a money back guarantee?" The quiet but very firm "NO!" answer stopped me in my tracks. I realized I had to look around to see if there were other*

alternatives out there for my own piece of mind.

"*<u>I work as an Investigator for the (state) Department of Consumer Affairs</u> and give this type of advice on a daily basis...* "*always get other estimates, know your alternatives and choices.*" *I started checking around the Internet. Through a discussion forum I saw Harj's program mentioned and went to the website. It was a blessing from heaven.*

"*With Harj's fair price on this system and webinars to help, I thought it's worth a try, and if it's not the same thing, I can always go back and pay the $3,500. Luckily I was able to get that $500 copycat deposit back and happily tried Harj's system. To my delight, I was the one controlling the program and inputting the data.*

"*I am able to get very specific and make changes when needed. I have spent hours playing with the numbers in the Speed Equity System and have found it to be incredibly accurate. I will have my home paid off in 4-years and 8-months and will be debt free!!!*

"*I really enjoy the ability to adjust my spending habits and see immediate results. I am now thrilled in doing my budgeting and seeing my savings reflected in reduced time and interest savings on my loan.*

"*Thanks Harj for your fairness, honesty and ingenious program!*"

> "*Most of the things worth doing in the world had been declared impossible before they were done.*"
>
> - Louis D. Brandeis -

SUMMARY

The SECRET to successfully achieving any goal in life is to make certain that you have a S.M.A.R.T. plan.

When my book was first launched in 1997, I observed many people rushing off and refinancing to a HELOC (Step 3) without having a plan to pay it back or the right tool to manage it properly. Six months later, they wondered why they still owed the bank the same amount of money they started with. This was not the fault of the bank, the HELOC, or this System. It was simply a case of people thinking they knew better, not willing to take responsibility to follow a proven System, let alone equipping themselves with the right HELOC management tool.

The reason your personalized Speed Equity® Plan is so critical is because it will act as your 'financial GPS' that will guide you in reaching your destination of Owning Your Home Years Sooner & Retiring Debt Free. I can categorically say that the best way for you to create the most accurate mortgage reduction plan for yourself is with the Speed Equity® Software program and ... *I've even created a way for you to get it for FREE!*

Furthermore, if you want to become financially wealthy or at least in a better position than where you are now, then the Speed Equity® Mortgage Acceleration System and Software is the best place to start. It not only gives you the theory but also the money management tool to help you do exactly what real life millionaires do, and that is to ...

> Allocate your time, energy and money efficiently in ways conducive to building wealth . . . as well as to BUDGET - AND - create a S.M.A.R.T. PLAN for you to own your most expensive asset - your home.

In conclusion, I hope that I have made my professional recommendation crystal clear in this chapter. And that is ...

> DO NOT GO ANY FURTHER WITH THE SPEED EQUITY® SYSTEM UNLESS YOU ARE ALSO WILLING TO CREATE AND MANAGE YOUR OWN PERSONALIZED SPEED EQUITY® PLAN, and you have the correct tool to do this properly.

"The indispensable first step to getting the things you want out of life is this: Decide what you want."

- Ben Stein -

Step 2: Chapter 15
How to Sabotage Proof Your HELOC
Using the Speed Equity® Mortgage Acceleration Software

*"Two roads diverged in a wood, and I – I took the one
less travelled by and that has made all the difference."*

- Robert Frost -

Remember with a HELOC, once you pay down your loan, you can withdraw ALL your funds right back out by either writing a check or by using your ATM card. Consequently, I have come across some people that have said to me:

"Harj, I love the results my Speed Equity® Software is showing me.

"However, it's too big a transition for me to deviate from what I've been used to by setting up my home loan as a day-to-day transaction account.

"Is there something I can do to achieve my forecasted results as well as protect myself - from myself - in the process?"

In other words, these people were unsure of whether they could keep their "hand out of the cookie jar" when withdrawing money for their monthly living expenses from their HELOC. The solution I always gave, and I give to you if you feel the same way, is to look at your forecasted budgeted living expenses for each month, as shown in the Speed Equity® Software's "Cashflow Summary Screen", and transfer that amount of money into a separate savings/checking account. Then, withdraw your monthly living expenses from *that* account ONLY.

You may ask; *"Doesn't that defeat the whole process of leaving all my money in the HELOC to reduce the daily balance and thereby reduce my interest cost?"*

Ans: Yes it does!

However, I deliberately designed the Software to have certain in-built, conservative assumptions that are in your favor. That is, if you do exactly what I have suggested (even though the best strategy is to leave all your funds sitting in your HELOC until you need them), you will still achieve your HELOC end of month forecasted Closing Balances as shown in the software. If you're skeptical, just trial it out and see for yourself.

The good news is that the Software is so accurate that it takes into account the FREQUENCY of all your regular expenses so you know exactly how much you are going to spend each month, and therefore, how much you need to transfer into a separate checking account if you want to sabotage proof your HELOC. For example, you know that not all your regular living expenses are incurred on a weekly, bi-weekly or monthly basis. In fact, some regular expenses come in every quarter, some half yearly and others yearly.

When inputting your data into the software, you can specify EXACTLY how much a particular regular expense is, the frequency with which it occurs as well as the month it is next due.

The Cash Flow Summary screen of the software then displays the fluctuating monthly regular expenses so that it accurately reflects what is happening in your "real" life AND then guides you on a month-by-month basis to achieve your forecasted HELOC Closing Balances (see Fig: 21 below).

Cash Flow Summary

H.E.L.O.C. As Primary	Jan	Feb	Mar	Apr
Original P&I Loan Balance	200001.00	199763.81	199427.52	199187.41
HELOC Balance	200001	199397.60	196669.11	194064.25
Heloc Credit Limit	300000.00	300000.00	300000.00	300000.00
HELOC Interest Rate	9%	9 %	9%	9%
Current HELOC Buffer Available	99999	100602.40	103330.89	105935.75
Regular Income				
Lump Sum Income				
TOTAL INCOME	3001.00	5002.00	50 .00	9 2.00
Regular Expenses	885.00	925.00	925.00	1425.00
Lump Sum Expenses	0.00	0.00	0.00	0.00
Current Debt Expenses	0.00	0.00	0.00	0.00
TOTAL EXPENSES	2135.00	2175.00	2175.00	2675.00

Take note of Regular Expenses for each month & transfer those funds to a separate savings/checking acct.

Fig. 21: Sabotage proofing your HELOC using the
Speed Equity® Mortgage Acceleration Software

*"There is nothing in the caterpillar
that tells you it's going to be a butterfly."*

- R. Buckmister Fuller -

SUMMARY

I don't want to discount the fact that sometimes it can seem like a gigantic step for some people to transition from an old habit to a new one, even if there are substantial gains to be had by adopting the new habit ... as is the case with using the Speed Equity® Mortgage Acceleration System.

The potential drawback some people feel when initially using this System is the temptation to keep dipping into the pot and spending the equity they have built up in their HELOC. Therefore, to accommodate the changeover, and to sabotage proof their HELOC, I recommend that people simply use the results from the Speed Equity® Mortgage Acceleration Software's "CashFlow Summary" screen.

That is, look at the FORECASTED Regular Expenses for each month, transfer those funds to a separate savings/checking account, and only withdraw money from that account.

Again, for the sabotage proofing strategy to work effectively, you must have the **FORECASTED Regular Expenses Results** from the software's "CashFlow Summary" screen.

> *"You have to take it as it happens, but you should*
> *try to make it happen the way you want to take it."*

> - German Proverb -

Step 3: Chapter 16
Getting The Right Loan

*"If you take responsibility for yourself you will
develop a hunger to accomplish your dreams."*

- Les Brown -

In this chapter, I am going to help you complete Step-3 by first describing the features you should look for in a "good" Home Equity Line of Credit (HELOC). Also included will be the location of the latest checklist of questions to ask a lender when you are ready to apply for one. Furthermore, I am going to recommend and assume that you are exercising Option-2 from Chapter 11 ("Making Wise Choices") by taking out a 'small' HELOC as a second mortgage to apply with the Speed Equity® Mortgage Acceleration System. Incidentally, I would highly recommend that you reread Chapter 11 before continuing.

 BEWARE: DON'T expect your lender to help you get the right HELOC ...

... that works with this System.

I already outlined in the "Read Me First" chapter why no lender, at the institutional level, would want to help you Own Your Home Years Sooner. I also know, from first hand experience, what you are going to face at the local branch level when you apply for your HELOC. I can tell you that you are going to meet a lot of blank faces, silly replies to your informed questions, and sometimes even downright contempt for what you are attempting to do. That's not because the bank staff are a part of some larger conspiracy, but because many are still ignorant about how this concept actually works.

For example, go to any bank's website and search for a Home Equity Line of Credit. You will notice they ALL market it for - and wait for it – vacations, buying a car, or remodeling your home. You will never see a HELOC marketed for use with a mortgage acceleration type of system because they simply don't know how to do it, nor would they want to promote it if they did. Furthermore, you will be challenging long held institutional paradigms that have never been questioned.

I have found that this is not an isolated case and happens continuously the world over wherever salespeople have a vested interest in selling you their products or services.

An intriguing tale of vested interest

When I first introduced this concept to the U.S. and Canada via the North American edition of this book in 2003, I gave a copy to my local bank branch manager. Immediately after she read it, she called me and said; *"This is brilliant. How can I work with you to introduce this to my clients?"*

We had several conference calls. Then she had several conference calls with her regional manager and finally got permission for me to run seminars at her branch. Pretty soon I had six branch managers from the same bank wanting me to run seminars at their locations. These seminars were so successful in bringing new clients into the branch and generated so much HELOC business that all six branch managers won an all expenses paid trip to Florida - with their spouses.

What happened after that?

Everyone was really excited thinking *"WOW, picking up new clients with this System is a complete no brainer and let's get full corporate support for it."*

Soon after, I was invited to Seattle, WA to meet with all the NW regional managers of this bank. That meeting was extremely unpleasant to say the least because they were all very hostile to introducing this concept to their corporate bosses. Needless to say, I walked away rather befuddled. I'm thinking; *"What's up with their attitude? They had phenomenally successful results from the six branch managers I had worked. They generated so much HELOC business with this System that they won a fully paid vacation, and yet, these regional managers were treating me as if I was some sort of pariah."*

At first, I thought it was the normal "lack of backbone syndrome" that middle managers have to introducing something to their superiors that is out of the box and having to take the rap in case things don't work out. The reality turned out to be much more sinister and self-serving. You see, this particular bank gave bonuses to their regional managers based on the amount of funds depositors kept in their checking accounts. As you now know, this System completely demolishes the bank's ability to make money off of your money because it makes your funds work much harder for you by funneling them through your HELOC instead of leaving them in your checking account thus ... bridging the gap between the interest they pay you as a depositor and the interest they charge you as a borrower.

Once I discovered the regional managers' "remuneration structure", it all made sense.

My decision from that day forward was to stop trying to convince major U.S. lenders that they should work with me and empower individual homeowners like you instead. So that's the long way of me saying, you have to take personal responsibility to get the right HELOC to make this System work because your lender is not going to help you do it. By the way, I'm more than happy to work with lenders. I'm just not going to waste my time dealing with middle level lackeys that are self-serving.

Incidentally, I was not invited to the Florida trip.

Now, let's get you started with ...

What to Look for in a 'Good' HELOC

These are the general features to look for:

- ❏ Set Up Costs … $0 to negligible*.
- ❏ Interest Rate Charges and Features ... competitive.
- ❏ Borrowing Limit … not too low.
- ❏ Loan Draw Period ... at least 10-years.
- ❏ Borrowing Terms and Conditions … flexible.
- ❏ Payment Terms and Conditions … no penalties for early payoff.
- ❏ Yearly maintenance fee … up to $90 per year is acceptable.

* NOTE: some lenders may charge an appraisal fee of $500 or more … based on the market value of your home.

EXTREMELY IMPORTANT

Make certain that you get a HELOC that matches your Speed Equity® Plan from Step-2.

"They are able because they think they are able."

\- Virgil -

Step 3: Chapter 17
What If You Can't Qualify For a HELOC?

"Hope doesn't come from calculating whether the
good news is winning out over the bad.
It's simply a choice to take action."

- Anna Lappe -

You're NOT alone

As of October 2016, *CoreLogic*'s latest *Equity Report* revealed that 91.1% of all U.S. mortgaged properties are now in a positive equity situation, while 75.9% now have significant equity *(defined as more than 20%)*! The report also revealed that 548,000 households regained equity in the second quarter of 2016 and are no longer under water.

However, if you are one of those homeowners that were "significantly" impacted by the 2008 financial crisis AND your home is still "underwater", that is, you still owe more on your mortgage than your house is currently worth, it means you probably won't be able to complete Step-3 of this System because you will most likely NOT qualify to get a HELOC to bring it to life.

So what can you do?

Ans: NEVER - EVER give up. And before you even get a tinge disheartened or upset thinking that you wasted your time reading this book, let's go back to basics by ...

Revisiting the right stuff to make this System work for you

All my coaching clients, including those I have referred to throughout this book had dreams that they thought would take years to fulfill ... mainly because of the mortgage hanging over their heads. However, EVERY single one of them who made the commitment to overcome this obstacle are now enjoying the lifestyle they had envisioned for themselves.

I have found through years of coaching experience that the one thing every single person who has Owned Their Home Years Sooner using this System has in common is a willingness to take charge of his or her life ... especially in the area of personal finance. And to back up my observations, I once again quote Drs. Stanley and Danko from their superbly researched book, *The Millionaire Next Door*. You see, one of the things they learned is that besides being frugal, persistent, and well educated ...

> " ... millionaires ARE NOT WORKAHOLICS, but finishers:
> they always complete their tasks or projects."

Now, doesn't that just about summarize the attributes you need to succeed in any endeavor in life? And that's exactly what I want for you ... i.e. to finish what you started to get on the road to Owning Your Home Years Sooner & retiring Debt FREE. On that note, and before I outline a solution for you, let me share with you ...

A story of hope and persistence

I'm sure you realize by now that what I have been proposing all along is NOT a quick fix solution. If you are truly serious about Owning Your Home Years Sooner & Retiring Debt Free using this System, then you know it requires you to take total control of not only your home loan, but also your personal finances.

Let me give you an example to illustrate what I mean.

Back in the day when I was consulting, a young couple, Simon & Fiona, came to see me and couldn't wait to get started. I soon found out that their abundant enthusiasm was the result of talking with friends for whom I had already coached and set up the System. All of their friends were doing nothing more than simply achieving the forecasted results in their Speed Equity® Plan - which, by the way, is always quite impressive to someone not familiar with what is possible with this System.

When I created their plan, the results showed that they could own their home in less than half of the time projected for their P&I loan - AND - they would save $84,847 in interest. You can only imagine how elated they were to hear this and couldn't wait to tell all of their friends that they too would soon be joining them on the fast track to home ownership.

What's more, I could see by their motivation that they would be real Spartans once they got started and would not only meet their projected goal of accelerated home ownership, but would most likely own their home a lot sooner than the time forecasted in their Speed Equity® Plan.

The only glitch was that they simply did not have enough equity in their home to get a HELOC to start the program at that time. What was even more disconcerting was that according to their loan repayments and the size of their mortgage, the calculations showed it would take them at least another three years before they would have enough equity to qualify for this type of loan.

You don't have to be a psychic to know that by the end of our session, the mood in the room was rather somber. Understandably, Simon & Fiona felt extremely frustrated and victimized. That's when I reminded them that *"life is a series of choices, and it's up to each of us to make wise choices."* So, we spent the next hour discussing some of the things they could do to build the equity in their home to bring down their LTV (loan to valuation ratio), so that they could qualify for a HELOC.

In summary, here's what they did:

✓ They took a good look at their spending habits, created a budget and cut down on some items that were not essential, such as getting take-out three nights a week, having cable TV with 500 channels, etc. I know that this last item is an essential for some people - akin to removing oxygen from the atmosphere, but these are some of the choices you may have to make. In Simon & Fiona's case, they used this 'surplus' money to make extra payments toward their P&I loan to bring down its balance, thus increasing the equity in their home.

✓ Next, they had several garage sales to get rid of the clutter in their home, and they also used this extra cash to inject into their P&I loan.

✓ They improved the value of their property by thousands of dollars with DIY projects like landscaping. This proved to be the most profitable return on their time and investment. Not only did they build equity in their home in record time, but it also kept them focused and working together as a couple toward a common goal, thus improving their personal relationship in the process.

✓ Finally, they 'borrowed' money from their parents, with a clear plan to pay it back, which they also injected into their P&I loan (see Chapter 12: "SECRETS to Using The Speed Equity® System to Save Even More Interest" for details on how they did this).

The great news is that this couple came back to see me eight months later and are living proof of the adage that 'necessity is the mother of all invention'. By doing all of the things we had discussed to build equity in their home, they not only qualified for a HELOC in record time and started on this System, but the financial management skills they learned in the process put them well on the road to Owning Their Home Years Sooner & Retiring Debt Free.

Therefore, if you are in a similar predicament as Simon & Fiona were, I can understand that it is aggravating. And I don't mean to preach here, but you, too, have a choice. You can either sit around stewing and moping, or you can use that e-Motion (energy-in-motion) by channeling it into constructive action. Be glad that you now know a much better way to pay off your mortgage, and then, simply do what Simon & Fiona did … make a commitment to take action. I guarantee that if you have half of the zeal they did, it won't take you long to get started with this System either.

Here's what I want you to do …

… if you know for a fact that you are still underwater on your mortgage …

… DO NOT follow through with Step 2 ("Creating Your Plan") just yet until you know that you have sufficient equity to qualify for a HELOC.

Next, I do want you to …

1. Go to www.**Speed**Equity**.com**
2. Click the "HELOC" tab (Top RHS); and ...
3. Use the LTV Calculator to assess how much equity you "may" have;
4. Contact a lender(s) to see if you can qualify for a HELOC.

PLEASE NOTE: Step-3 ("Getting The Right HELOC") is completely beyond my control as it involves a third party. Therefore, if you can't qualify for a HELOC just yet, you will have to take charge of your situation and create your own plan of action, just like the couple in the Case Example I just gave you.

Last, let this be your mantra ...

> *"Enthusiasm is the greatest asset in the world.*
> *It beats money and power and influence."*

> - Henry Chester -

Chapter 18
Retiring Debt Free

*"Twenty years from now you will be more disappointed
by the things you didn't do than by the things you did.
So throw off the bowlines. Sail away from the safe harbor.
Catch the winds in your sails.
Explore. Dream."*

- Mark Twain -

Let's finish up with the sub-title of this book in terms of Retiring Debt Free.

As I said in Chapter 1 ("Why You Should Own Your Home Years Sooner As An American"), my desire is that you go way beyond the immediate goal of accelerated home ownership and become financially independent as well. In order to do that, you have to have the right financial tools to help you. But first, let me address one of *the* most common questions I am always asked. And that is ...

Should you pay off your mortgage first - OR - purchase an investment vehicle?

What I am about to reveal to you tics off a lot of Financial Planners/ Advisors/Consultants/Brokers (you fill in the title here). In fact, in the past I have come under attack from some of the people in these occupations. That's because their vested interest is to sell you their financial products, and when you direct your income to Owning Your Home Years Sooner, they feel their livelihoods being threatened ... and of course they see me as the villain leading the charge.

Whenever I speak to people from these professions, I have to take a deep breath and educate them about the most basic fundamentals of investing. I begin by telling them that I'm not here to rain on anyone's parade. My primary goal is to help people make the best possible decision about how to allocate their hard earned money by first and foremost, EDUCATING them ... which is what they should be doing.

I tell them, in order to truly assess whether your clients should put their money toward Owning Their Homes Years Sooner or purchasing an investment vehicle is to examine that question in terms of the following Key Principle. And that is ...

> ## KEY PRINCIPAL
> SAVING Interest is THE SAME as EARNING Interest.

In terms of ROI, if you use your money to SAVE interest on your mortgage, then that is exactly the same as EARNING that amount of interest. The best part is that you DON'T have to pay tax on the interest you SAVE whereas you would have to pay tax on any interest/ returns you EARN (regardless of whether you put that money in an interest bearing account or an investment vehicle). For example, let's say you have a $250,000 mortgage at 4% and $10,000 cash in a savings account set aside for renovations, or a holiday, or whatever.

In most instances you can expect to earn about 0.5 percent, or less, on the $10,000 sitting in the savings account and then, you have to report that income to the IRS -AND- you have to pay tax on it at your marginal tax rate because you would EARN interest. Meanwhile, you are paying 4 percent interest on your mortgage (see Fig. 22 below).

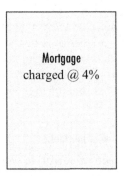

Fig. 22: The gap between what you EARN in interest & what you usually PAY on your mortgage.

Mortgage charged @ 4%

Savings Acct. earns 0.5%

Keeping in mind our Key Principle, let me ask you, would you rather EARN 0.5 percent in interest on your $10,000 or would you rather SAVE 4 percent in interest by putting it toward your mortgage?

In our example, if you leave that $10,000 in a normal savings account earning 0.5 percent, you would EARN $50 after 12-months. And remember, the real ROI is even less because you would have to pay tax on the $50 you earn. If you're in the 30% tax bracket, that $50 shrivels down to a "real" AFTER-TAX ROI of $35 … NOT factoring in inflation.

On the other hand, if you were to inject that same $10,000 into your mortgage, you would SAVE $400 in interest after 12-months. So your ROI would be more than 8-fold on the same amount of money. The best part is, because you would be SAVING interest as opposed to EARNING interest ... **YOU WON'T HAVE TO REPORT**, let alone pay any tax on the $400 interest you save!

Having said that, the reason people don't "park" their money in their mortgage is because most mortgages are simple P&I loans that lock in your payments and it costs thousands of dollars in refinancing fees to get your money back out. However, as I have taught you, with a HELOC, your money is available at call and doesn't cost you anything to access it. And until you do, your money is working much, much harder for you compared to sitting in a standard savings or checking account.

I then supplement with the following decision making process ... I tell them, whenever dealing with your clients, shouldn't you ALWAYS present your proposition using the following three (3) interconnected variables so your clients can make the best possible informed decision (Fig. 23 below)?

Fig. 23: Simple decision making matrix for assessing investments.

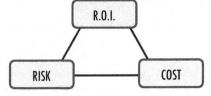

Now that we've assessed the real ROI of your clients putting their money toward Owning Their Home Years Sooner vs. directing it into an investment vehicle you want to sell them, let's take a look at the ...

COST: of getting into your investment. I'm sure you've heard of fund managers offering 10 or 12 percent ROI, but once you take into account all the fees, charges, and commissions, your initial investment amount may shrivel down by several thousand dollars. Therefore, the "real" ROI on our $10,000 may end up being even less regardless of whether these costs are taken out at the front end, or the back end (i.e., after the ROI is paid at maturity). Next, we have to examine the ...

RISK: associated with the investment. Unfortunately, I have seen investors get bamboozled into handing over their hard earned money because of promises of sensational ROIs - and end up losing it ALL. The main reason is that they fail to ask a very important question, and that is; *"What is the risk associated with this investment?"* In the case of Bernie Madoff's clients, they didn't want to know as long as they kept getting their cut.

I won't go into the psychological reasons as to why people don't ask this obvious question but suffice to say that there is a systematic way you can reduce your chances of getting burned. Here are some basic guidelines to help you:

- History: Find out how long the company has been around? Obviously, the longer the company has been in business, the more history you have to carry out your due diligence with.

- Ask for testimonials: from people that have invested in the opportunity. However, testimonials can also be "slanted" to give an overly rosy and false picture. So please be careful unless you know the people providing the testimonials personally. If there are thousands of people getting great results - especially over an extended period of time - then obviously it "MAY" be a good thing.

- Expert Reviews: Technically speaking, this is the best form of endorsement because experts are "supposed" to provide in-depth, impartial analysis. Quite frankly, I've seen too many of these so-called "financial gurus" that appear regularly on TV spewing out advice, and yet, did you notice that not a single one of them predicted the housing and economic collapse of 2008? Personally, I think most of them have sold out. And all you have to do is follow the money trail to see who and what they are endorsing to figure out if they're really impartial.

In conclusion, whenever analyzing whether you should use your discretionary income to purchase an investment vehicle or use it to Own Your Home Years Sooner, you can approach the situation in exactly the same way as our example (i.e., should you park your money in your mortgage or a savings account OR purchase an investment vehicle?).

If the ROI being offered is more than what you can get compared to the interest savings on your mortgage, and the Cost, and RISK is acceptable to you, then by all means go ahead. However, now you have a working template with which to make that assessment.

Let me conclude by briefly outlining how the Speed Equity® Mortgage Acceleration System sets you up for wealth creation - and at the very least, to be able to Retire Debt Free.

Using The Speed Equity® System to become AND stay debt free for life

I can categorically say that a HELOC is by far one of *the* best monetary tools that you can have at your disposal. That's because once you set up a HELOC, in most cases, it can be a lifelong credit facility. That means you can access your money right up to the original credit limit, at any time, for any purpose, at call and then use the Speed Equity® Mortgage Acceleration System to pay for the acquisition exactly as you would to pay off your home.

For example, let's say you decide to spend $30,000 as a Lump Sum Expense to update your car in 5-years time. In most cases, when people need money for this type of expense, they either save up for it, or take out a Personal or a Car Loan - which usually has a higher interest rate than the prevailing interest rate for a HELOC. But with a HELOC, you can withdraw the $30,000 by simply writing a cheque from it and then use the Speed Equity® System to own it years sooner.

The benefits of this option are:

a. You will NEVER have to see a bank manager for loan approval ever again.

b. You will NEVER have to pay for new loan set-up costs ever again (i.e. application fee).

c. You will SAVE MONEY because the prevailing interest rates for HELOCs are always lower than the interest rates for Personal Loans (in most cases).

This is in contrast to P&I loans, which have a fixed amortization schedule and require you to re-apply for finance whenever you need a new loan, which of course costs you money in the form of origination fees.

Using the Speed Equity® System as a wealth creation tool

Let me share with you a quick example from one of my coaching clients that used a HELOC and this System superbly well to start accumulating income-generating assets. By the way, these clients were certainly NOT millionaires. They were just ordinary folk that learned to work smarter with their money.

After several years of using this System, these clients had built up a significant amount of equity in their home. They then decided to buy an investment property and found one they liked. Because they had their money available at call via their HELOC, they made an offer to the seller for $35,000 less than the asking price for the property.

They said to the vendor; *"If you accept our offer RIGHT NOW, we can have the cheque to you first thing tomorrow morning."* The seller accepted their offer on the spot and these clients instantly saved/made $35,000. That is the bargaining power available to people who know how to use this fantastic financial product properly. They then used the Speed Equity® System to own their investment property years sooner as well.

Would you say that in this instance, they certainly **ALLOCATED THEIR TIME, ENERGY, AND MONEY EFFICIENTLY IN WAYS CONDUCIVE TO BUILDING WEALTH?** And you too will be able to do the same if you manage your HELOC properly as I have been describing by using the Speed Equity® Mortgage Acceleration Software.

"The greatest obstacle to discovery is NOT ignorance but the illusion of knowledge."

- Daniel J. Boorstin -

SUMMARY

To summarize this chapter, I'm not here to give you a long monologue about how to invest because that's not what this book is about. My primary objective is to get you started on getting rid of the single, largest debt you have by teaching you how make more effective and efficient use of your existing financial resources. Along the way, I hope you have picked up some fundamental money management principles that will serve you well when you are ready to take the next step to invest all that equity you're going to accumulate in rapid time.

On that note, I can give you some simple guidelines that I myself use to figure out if an investment opportunity is any good ... especially when compared to Owning Your Home Years Sooner. Therefore, you can - and should - ask the following questions whenever you're presented with an investment opportunity:

1. What's the ROI?
2. What's the real ROI - (i.e., after tax)?
3. What's the COST associated with getting into the investment opportunity?
4. What's the RISK?

You can then use the answers from the above questions to compare ...

The benefits of using your money to Own Your Home Years Sooner:

- **ROI:** is whatever interest your mortgage is being charged. In our example it was 4 percent.
- **The Real ROI:** was also 4 percent because NO TAX is paid on the interest you save.
- **The Real ROI is IMMEDIATE:** You will start saving interest from the moment you inject your money into your mortgage because the interest on it ... wait for it ... is calculate on the daily balance.
- **COST:** there is absolutely $0 cost to get this ROI.
- **RISK:** The only risk is YOU. That is, if you've created your personalized Speed Equity® Plan and don't stick to it, you only have yourself to blame. There is no other risk other than the entire financial system crashing, in which case, we're all up the proverbial creek without a paddle.
- **Liquidity:** YOU have total control of YOUR money at ALL times and YOU can ALWAYS access it via your HELOC at any time.

"Facts do not cease to exist because they are ignored."

- Aldus Huxley -

The Final Word

"All the time, Destiny is within one's grasp.
Through action. Determined, committed action."

- William James Scully -

Just take a moment to imagine having the freedom to do all of the things you want to do when your mortgage is no longer a ball-and-chain burden in your life.

That would be wild, wouldn't it?

Or alternatively, think about saving enough interest that it's equivalent to a full year's salary. Imagine what you could do with all that money.

Now I know from personal experience that, at this stage, you may feel somewhat overwhelmed. You may be saying to yourself, *"Could this really work for me?"* Or, *"Am I really going to save that much time & interest?"*

In response, all I can say to you is what I used to say to all my coaching clients, and that is, **numbers don't lie**. What's more, neither of us will know how much time and interest you could save unless you follow through with Step-2 and create your own personalized Speed Equity® Plan.

Having said that, I also appreciate that changing the way you think about paying off your home loan may be somewhat daunting. You had to do a lot of running around to get your current P&I loan. It was a stressful and time-consuming procedure. And just when everything is running smoothly, the last thing you feel like doing is to repeat that ordeal. Although … **NONE of that is necessary when applying for your HELOC (Step-3) because it's a much easier process!**

Furthermore, you may have even tried to discuss this concept with family & friends and received negative feedback. I guarantee the first thing some of them will have said is, *"Oh yeah, I've heard about this concept and … I read somewhere that it doesn't work or it's a scam."*

Whenever you get such a response, which will be often, don't try to get into a debate. Just remember the distinction I made between skeptics and cynics. **Be aware that neither of them will have read this book - especially the cynics.** That means you now know a lot more than the general population about how to eliminate your mortgage years sooner, including most bankers. For example, how many people can talk intelligently to you about:

- *How interest is calculate and charged on a home loan? Or,*
- *How lenders make their profits using fractional-reserve banking? Or,*
- *The effect of compound interest in creating a Prison Made From Pennies?*
- *I could go on …*

The point I want to make is that you will meet a lot of cynics that are persistent in pushing their ignorance about this idea. In which case, just ask yourself this one simple question; *"Are they Owning Their Homes Years Sooner and saving tens of thousands of dollars in interest on their mortgage?"* I assure you the answer will be a resounding "NO". Therefore, my recommendation to you is …

Let your life be your prayer

This is the advice a very wise friend once gave me, and I endeavor to live by it every day. He also said to me, *"Harj, if you want to be successful, hang around with successful people."* Have you noticed that this axiom is spot on? So in turn, my advice to you is don't listen to negative chatter, including the stuff in your head. Just as important, don't hang around with cynics who say you can't do this or it doesn't work. That brings me to my next point. I've found there's safety in numbers.

Let me explain.

I visited an old friend at his workplace because he was really eager to introduce me to all his coworkers. He said once he had set up his Speed Equity® Plan and saw how much time and interest he would save, he started telling everyone else in the office about it. Pretty soon they were all talking about this System and collectively helped each other to create their own personalized plans and now, they're all doing great. I was really humbled because his colleagues wanted to meet me in person just to say "thank you".

That encounter led me to create …

The Speed Equity® "Employee Benefit Program"

If you're reading this as a result of your employer's participation in this program, I encourage you to start your own mini movement among your colleagues and support each other in achieving your monthly goals. **I also invite you to join my PRIVATE Facebook group** where you will find like-minded individuals that are more than willing to share their interest saving tips & strategies.

My friend said that the best thing he could do to help others was to share what he was doing successfully in his own life. He went on to say, *"My monthly loan statements are living proof that my plan is working for me."* He is also on his way to owning his second investment property.

Tell me, how can you argue against that?

By the way, I forgot to mention one of the most important points and that is …

What have you got to lose?

I've designed this System so that it's easy to understand and apply, and if you follow the three steps as I have outlined, you too can be well on your way to saving tens to hundreds of $1,000's in interest and Owning Your Home Years Sooner & Retiring Debt Free.

As I explained in Chapter 12 ("SECRETS to Using the Speed Equity® System to Save Even More Interest"), if you setup this System and apply the credit card interest saving strategy just once, in that example, I proved how you could save a whopping $19,116.99.

> Tell me, where else can you get a GUARANTEED ROI like that at $0 cost to you?

Allow me to share with you a life-changing article I read

On February 1st, 2012, **"The Guardian"** newspaper in Britain ran a story titled; *"Top five regrets of the dying."* It was about an Australian nurse by the name of Bronnie Ware who spent several years working in palliative care. In her tenure of caring for patients in the last weeks of their lives, she recorded the most common regrets of her dying patients and put her findings in a blog called; *"Inspiration and Chai"*.

She discovered that people gain a phenomenal sense of clarity at the end of their lives and said we can learn from their wisdom. She is quoted; *"When questioned about any regrets they had or anything they would do differently,"* she said, *"common themes surfaced again and again."*

Ware said the **two most common regrets people have are** - and I quote directly from the article ...

Regret #1: I WISH I HAD the courage to live a life true to myself

"This was the most common regret of all. When people realise that their life is almost over and look back clearly on it, it is easy to see how many dreams have gone unfulfilled. Most people had not honoured even a half of their dreams and had to die knowing that it was due to choices they had made, or not made. Health brings a freedom very few realise, until they no longer have it."

Regret #2: I WISH I HADN'T worked so hard

"This came from EVERY male patient that I nursed. They missed their children's youth and their partner's companionship. Women also spoke of this regret, but as most were from an older generation, many of the female patients had not been breadwinners. All of the men I nursed deeply regretted spending so much of their lives on the treadmill of a work existence."

In this day and age when so many women are breadwinners also, I would venture to say that when our generation reaches its flickering twilight moment, equal numbers of men AND women will have this regret.

It's NEVER TOO LATE to live a life WITHOUT REGRET

Let me ask you, how many dreams do you have that are yet unrealized? And how many of those dreams could you start fulfilling right now if you knew you could be mortgage and debt free years sooner?

The Speed Equity® System gives you the knowledge, tools and resources to do exactly that by allocating your time, energy and money efficiently in ways conducive to building wealth.

It's not some nebulous concept.

It gives you real, tangible, actionable steps that you can implement today.

It puts full RESPONSE-ABILITY in your hands so you can be RESPONSE-ABLE to create a desirable financial future for you and your loved ones.

You don't have to work harder to earn extra money to make it work. You don't have to win the Lotto. You don't have to be funneled onto a seminar treadmill. You might not become a millionaire as a result of using this System, but by golly you're sure going to be a lot better off financially than where you are right now.

Can you see how easy this System makes it for you to start working SMARTER with the money you have right now rather than working harder? This is such a worthy thing you can do for yourself, your family, your health and your sanity. Besides …

There is a much bigger purpose here because …

I wholeheartedly believe that we are ALL generous beings.

I believe we inherently want to give to others in need and … the world certainly needs more givers today. However, most families are unable to do that because they are so burdened with their own financial predicament. That's why I so urgently want you to use this System to get the single most oppressive debt off of your shoulders so it enables you to be more giving.

I want to conclude this book with a deeply personal confession

I'd like to share something with you that I do not reveal to many people. And that is, I wish I could go back in time and teach my parents about this System.

You see, I'm the oldest of four siblings and we were all born in Malaysia. When I was eleven years old, my parents made a life changing decision to migrate to Australia to give us a better life … that's where I grew up.

We were what you would call "working class folk". Both my parents worked three jobs each. My father was a diesel mechanic during the day and he earned a little extra money by repairing people's cars in the evening.

My mother cleaned office buildings from 6pm to 10pm. She would then go to her second job in a meatpacking factory where she worked the graveyard shift on an assembly line until 6am after which … she rushed home, got us ready for school, made sure all the housework was done while we were gone, made dinner and tried to get some rest before we got back home. On the weekends, my parents had a food vending truck that the whole family helped out with.

It was a hard, arduous existence because my parents' dream was to pay off their mortgage and be debt free as fast as humanly possible so they could focus on providing us with a good education. An opportunity they were not accorded in our former country of residence.

As a result, we never went on a vacation and no one read any bedtime stories.

For me the worst time was Christmas.

In fact I hated it.

Christmas Down Under takes place during the southern summer months when all the kids are out of school. So when we all returned the following year, everyone was excited to talk about what gifts they received. I was always embarrassed and dreaded being asked that question. There were not many presents to go around in the Gill household.

Through all this, I never heard my parents complain about having to work as hard as they did ... not once.

Our life in Australia was much, much better than the one we left behind in Malaysia. And like most immigrant families, we were extremely grateful for it.

My parents thought that having the opportunity and freedom to work three jobs to provide for our family and be able to give us a good education was like having Christmas every day.

I wish I could go back in time and teach them about this System so they didn't have to work so hard. Perhaps they could have become mortgage and debt free years sooner. Perhaps we could have had dinner like a normal family every evening. Perhaps they could have read us bedtime stories. Perhaps I would have followed a completely different path in life if all those things had come to fruition and ... this book would have never been written.

So please ... don't take this confession as a weep fest.

My experiences have made me the person I am today and I like me. I learned the value of thrift, responsibility, sacrifice and hard work from my parents. I appreciate what they did for us.

The reason I want to reveal all this to you is because I too am a parent now. My daughter is ten years old and it seems like only yesterday that I was changing her diapers and cradling her to sleep on my belly. I don't ever want to miss out on being a part of her life and watching her grow up. So when people ask me why I'm so passionate about what I do, I tell them ...

> **"Because this is not a job for me ... IT'S A MISSION!"**

Right now, there's a family out there with young children wishing that their parents could spend more time with them instead of working so hard. There are parents wishing they could do the same with their kids. It's too late for me until someone invents time travel. But until then, I console myself with paying it forward the best way I know how, and that is by teaching as many families about this System as I can.

In closing, I say to you, please, please don't let this book be just another one you read about financial freedom and then put it on the shelf because … you have the power right this moment to make the RESPONSE-ABLE choice to Own Your Home Years Sooner & Retire Debt Free.

The average amount of time people are saving with this System is 16-years and the average interest saving is $109,293.

The very least you can do is find out how much you could save by taking Step-2 because you just …

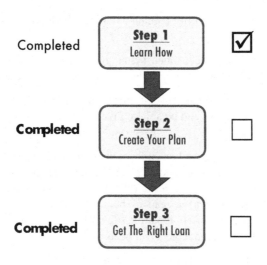

"Do or DO NOT.
There is no try."
- Yoda -

About the author

Harj Gill is an International Mortgage Reduction Expert & Bestselling Author of, *"How to Own Your Home Years Sooner & Retire Debt FREE"*. He is also the CEO of Speed Equity®, LLC.

Academically, he is trained as a research analyst and organizational consultant. He has a Bachelor of Science degree from the University of Western Australia as well as a Postgraduate Diploma in Science and a Masters Degree in Education.

Since 1995 Harj has dedicated his life to educating homeowners about a revolutionary mortgage acceleration concept he calls the Speed Equity® System. This System is designed to quickly build a homeowner's equity and help them pay off their mortgage faster than any other mortgage acceleration strategy available.

Leading Financial Experts and publications including **"Personal Investment Magazine"** and **"The Sunday Times"** have given Harj's Speed Equity® System and book rave reviews. **NBC's "Saving You Money"** said; *"... it's a BRILLIANT System."*

Harj is certified as a continuing education clock hour instructor for real estate agents with the **WASHINGTON State Department of Licensing (WADOL)** (Instructor ID#: 13851) as well as being a certified Administrator of the Speed Equity® School of Real Estate (School ID# S1705).

His "Mortgage Acceleration" Clock Hour Course (ID# C7037) is the only one of its kind in the entire country that has been approved by a formal government body and is available to real estate agents in WA - with this book being used as a reference.

In 2013, Harj obtained his real estate license so he could help homebuyers anywhere in the U.S. to get started with the Speed Equity® System at $0 cost.

He currently resides in WASHINGTON State with his wife and daughter.

His passion ... ADDING to Life & raising his daughter to be a Global Citizen.

His mission ... to help people become Mortgage AND Debt free YEARS SOONER.

His favorite past time ... cooking for family & friends.

His favorite saying ...

> ### "Let your Life be your Prayer."

You can reach him via eMail: Contact@SpeedEquity.com

Made in the USA
Columbia, SC
02 June 2021